Work
and
the Nature of Man

Frederick Herzberg
PROFESSOR OF PSYCHOLOGY
WESTERN RESERVE UNIVERSITY

THOMAS Y. CROWELL, PUBLISHERS
ESTABLISHED 1834
NEW YORK

Grateful acknowledgment is made to the publishers
who have granted permission to use the following material:

From A MAN FOR ALL SEASONS, by Robert Bolt.
© Copyright 1962 by Robert Bolt. Reprinted by permission
of Random House, Inc.

From JOB ATTITUDES IN THE SOVIET UNION, by
Frederick Herzberg, in Vol. 18, No. 3, of *Personnel Psychology*.

From KNOWLEDGE FOR WHAT? by Robert Lynd. © Copyright
1939 by Princeton University Press. Reprinted by
permission of Princeton University Press.

From THE MOTIVATION HYGIENE CONCEPT AND PROBLEMS OF
MANPOWER, by Frederick Herzberg, in Jan.–Feb. 1964
issue of *Personnel Administration*. By permission.

From A MOTIVATION-HYGIENE CONCEPT OF MENTAL HEALTH.
With permission from Industrial Relations Counselors,
Inc., New York; see *Behavioral Science Research in Industrial
Relations*, Industrial Relations Monograph, No. 21, 1962, p. 38.

From MOTIVATION TO WORK, 2nd Ed., by Herzberg, Mausner
and Schneiderman. © Copyright John Wiley and Sons.
New York, 1959. By permission of authors and publisher.

Library of Congress catalog card number: 65–27422

Printed in the United States of America

Published in Canada by Fitzhenry & Whiteside Limited, Toronto

ISBN 0–690–00371–4

8   9   10

To
Shirley
and
Mark

SIR THOMAS MORE: But Richard . . . Why not be a teacher? You'd be a fine teacher. Perhaps even a great one.

RICHARD: And if I was, who would know it?

SIR THOMAS: You, your pupils, your friends, God. Not a bad public that . . .

—Robert Bolt, *A Man for All Seasons*

Preface

WORK AND THE NATURE OF MAN is the third book of a trilogy concerning job attitudes. In the first book, *Job Attitudes: Review of Research and Opinion,* my colleagues and I attempted to review and systematize what had been gleaned from research and contemplation after a half-century of effort. In the *Motivation to Work* that followed, we described an original research study that offered a completely new hypothesis about the way people feel about their jobs. In this book, I have taken that hypothesis and expanded it to a general theory of Work and the Nature of Man. While the trilogy contains the three basic stages of scientific inquiry, knowledge of what has gone before, new research and finally a theory, the task that I set out for myself many years ago, upon graduation from the School of Public Health at the University of Pittsburgh, is just beginning. That task was to give original substance to the new discipline of Industrial Mental Health and, if possible, to make some positive contributions.

This third study is a specific product of more than four years of participation in a multitude of management programs all over the nation and in many parts of Europe. Initially, these programs served to explain and expand on the significance of the motivation-hygiene theory of job attitudes, first published in *The Motivation to Work* (1959). The task of summarizing the findings of the book to management audiences consists mainly in setting the play-back needle on one's brain and letting the vocal chords take over. It does not take long to discover the old truism that explaining to others leads to explaining to oneself.

A relatively neat package of research that stood on acceptable scientific grounds became in the process of explaining—and reacting to questions from the audience—a seemingly new look at the understanding of the motivation of people on jobs. An entirely new hypothesis emerged in the process of generalizing from job-motivation theory to actual problems faced by industry.

If ever the marriage between academic research and practical experience bore fruit, it did so in these excursions to address business groups. Management discovered that the behavioral scientists were asking questions that concerned them from both the business and human aspects; and the behavioral scientists came to recognize the data as applying to human beings rather than to abstract criteria of functioning beings. In this meshing of managers and behavioral scientists, the scientists became aware of their presumption in promising to industry benefits that managers themselves could achieve *infinitely* better.

Here I am speaking of the direct (or implied) promise of increased productivity and profits that can be attained if the advice tendered by social scientists is followed. The fact is that the increase in profits that the psychologists can effect at any one time is slight in comparison with the effects of the engineers, marketing experts and sales department. This is not to minimize the proven practical results of psychological understanding and psychological tools, but my experiences have demonstrated to me that managers and other workers, while seeking practical help with business problems, are also eager to learn from psychologists what their own jobs and lives are about. This seems a more warranted and valid area for investigation and study by behavioral scientists.

There has been in the past few decades a silent revolution in which man is protesting not merely the treatment society accords him but the very conception of his nature as it has been fostered by the prevailing institutions. He seems to demand a more realistic appraisal of his nature than the myths about him that have so conveniently and over so long a period been provided. If the past centuries have seen man shift from a mystical to a rational point of view of his physical universe, he now demands an equally rational view of his total needs.

From the most primitive of beginnings, man has hunted as relentlessly and unceasingly for explanations concerning the meaning of life as he has sought food and shelter. This never-ending quest reflects the persistent and optimistic nature of mankind—the need to alleviate man's existential terrors by finding a purpose for being.

Unfortunately, the knowledge man has obtained about the human condition continues to fall far behind his phenomenal progress in solving problems in his environment. At least the tentative answers to the questions about human nature have not been accepted. The impatience with which a materially flourishing society views speculations on human nature might be one cause for this failure. Perhaps the philosopher's preoccupation with the verities of existence smacks too much of medieval metaphysics for the Space-Age man.

That may be the reason why industry, the child prodigy of rationality and science, has increasingly assumed a leadership role in the search for solutions to the problems of man's psychological needs, in addition to its concern with satisfying man's physical needs. For these reasons industry invites the psychologist to participate in planning sessions about human behavior. So enmeshed has industry been with the answers to the human problems arising in that sphere of life that even the imperfect advice offered by the social scientists has frequently been accepted, in part if not in total, with the appropriate disclaimers and criticisms from both industrialists and scientists.

Essentially, industry has demanded that the behavioral scientist bulwark the image of rationality associated with the modern concept of commerce by giving a scientific aura to the management force. This purposeful use of social science has been made in an attempt to equalize the scientific advances with the complex technological development of administrative procedures.

Unhappily, to some managers it does not seem to matter whether the techniques of the behavioral scientists prove valid or not. What appears to be more important to them is that they are fulfilling their obligations to humanity by dealing with the

Geist of human behavior in a manner consistent with industry's image of science and reason.

It seems clear that industry, as the dominant institution of our society, profits from the imperfect answers about human nature and its needs that have been purveyed by the practitioners of my profession. Furthermore, these incomplete answers about human behavior have already proven to be the most necessary tools in the building of the modern industrial monolith.

Although society speaks of man's achieving his potential, we are actually retarding human achievement. The problem of achievement (or present lack of it) is central to the subject of this essay. Industry must realize that it is one of the despoilers of man's efforts to achieve happiness—in spite of management's most sincere attempts to do just the opposite. This phenomenon must be understood and investigated; it is a basic question with which industry must come to grips. My task is to offer a definition of man's total needs, one that is consistent within the world of work.

I admit to an overriding interest in mental health (a woolly term to which I hope to give some substantive meaning within the text), because it seems to me that mental health is the core issue of our times. And, after four years on the management training rostrums, I believe that people in management are in tacit agreement with me.

The primary functions of any organization, whether religious, political or industrial, should be to implement the needs for man to enjoy a meaningful existence. For the first time in history we have the opportunity to satisfy man's inherent wants. Yet what value to man if industry manufactures commodities to supply material comfort at the expense of human development and happiness?

My second purpose in writing this sequel to *The Motivation to Work* is that the job-attitude theory presented in that book has led to a gratifying number of studies designed to replicate and test the validity of the theory. Sufficient new data is now available to justify more confidence in the theory, so that this essay will also provide a means by which to review the follow-up studies. Also, it will enable me to clarify some of the more ob-

As a common ground for demonstration and discussion, Professor Herzberg presents his motivation-hygiene theory (a definition of man's total needs) as a solution to the problems facing management today, and urgently suggests that while industry has satisfied man's *outer wants* with those material things necessary to the "good life" it has lost sight of the *inner needs* necessary for a man's creative survival.

Work and the Nature of Man is a comprehensive report on research related to the motivation-hygiene theory in major industrial, institutional, and academic settings in the United States and in foreign countries. It is also a testimony to the effectiveness of one man's ideas in reshaping the concept of business itself.

☐ Frederick Herzberg is professor of psychology at Western Reserve University in Cleveland and lecturer in preventative medicine at the University of Oklahoma. A graduate of the City College of New York (B.S.S.), the University of Pittsburgh (M.S., Ph.D.), and the Pittsburgh Graduate School of Public Health (M.P.H.), he was the recipient of a Fulbright Fellowship to Finland in 1964. Currently a consultant for the American Institute of Research, the Veterans Administration, and numerous industrial, educational, and government organizations, Dr. Herzberg is the author of *The Motivation to Work and Job Attitudes.*

Jacket design and photo by Milton Charles

Thomas Y. Crowell Company
Established 1834
10 E. 53d Street
New York, New York 10022

scure points in the theory as well as correct some misinterpretations.

With the expansion of the theory as the result of new evidence and of the challenges that have accompanied my presentations to management, I have found myself far from my own discipline. I must therefore disclaim any special knowledge and understanding in the other areas in which I roam in the text. These include not only disciplines outside of psychology but also the subspecialities that are, for some strange reason, all tenants in the house of psychology.

If this discourse sounds too neat, and too full of loose ends, I plead guilty to exploring—this book has been a means of establishing new landmarks for me as I wander and wonder. What I mean is not exactly what I have written. As T. S. Eliot has Sweeney explain it: "I've gotta use words when I talk to you."

Acknowledgments

Mrs. Joanne Kaufman has been my assistant throughout the preparation and writing of this book. I am in great debt to this remarkable and talented woman.

I would also like to express my gratitude to Dr. Robert Ford and Mr. Roy Walters of the American Telephone and Telegraph Company, who have given reality to the motivation-hygiene theory in so many imaginative ways within the Bell System. I am grateful also for their continuing friendship.

To the thousands of managers in the following organizations my thanks and apologies: American Telephone and Telegraph Company, Bell Laboratories, B. F. Goodrich, British Petroleum (London), British American Tobacco (London), Bureau of Indian Affairs, Caterpillar Tractor, Civil Service Commission, Chesapeake and Potomac Bell Telephone, Dominion Tar and Chemical (Montreal), Eastman Kodak, Electric Storage Battery, Federal Aviation Agency, Ferry Nut and Screw, Forest City, General Motors, Hyatt, Imperial Chemical (London), Imperial Tobacco (Montreal), International Business Machines, LaBatt Breweries (Canada), Michigan Bell Telephone, Nationwide Insurance, Pacific Northwest Bell Telephone, Phillips (Eindhoven, Netherlands), Radio Corporation of America Laboratories, Sandia, Serlachius O Y (Finland), Standard Oil of Ohio, Texas Instruments,

Trans-Canada Airlines, Union Bag-Camp Paper, Univac, and Western Electric.

Finally, to the many professional organizations and academic institutions which invited me to address them over the years, my sincere thanks for the gentleness of their criticisms.

FREDERICK HERZBERG

Contents

Preface   vii

Chapter 1
Business—Dominant Institution of Modern Times   1

Chapter 2
Adam and Abraham   12

Chapter 3
Industry's Concepts of Man   32

Chapter 4
The Basic Needs of Man   44

Chapter 5
Psychological Growth   57

Chapter 6
The Motivation-Hygiene Theory   71

Chapter 7
Verification of the Theory of Motivation-Hygiene   92

Chapter 8
Further Verification of the Motivation-Hygiene Theory   130

Chapter 9
What Do We Do?   168

Appendix   193

References   199

Tables

I

Types of Adjustments   88

II

Characteristics of Hygiene and Motivation Seekers   90

III

Populations in 10 Tests of Motivation-Hygiene Theory of
Job Attitudes   122

IV

Summary of Factors Which Showed Significant Differences
Between Positive and Negative Incidents of Job Feelings
Representing 10 Studies of 17 Populations   124

V

525 Male Nonsupervisors   138

VI

131 Female Nonsupervisors   138

VII

Response of Male Nonsupervisors   139

VIII

Hospital Events (First Level)   142

IX
Hospital Events (Second Level)   143

X
Job Events (First Level)   143

XI
Job Events (Second Level)   143

XII
Relationship Between Individual Motivations and
Job Characteristics   144

XIII
Percent of Total Responses Excluding Unscorable
Schizophrenic Responses   153

XIV
Relationship of Motivational Pattern to Improvement
in Rehabilitation   157

XV
Relationship of Work Motivations to Improvement
in Rehabilitation   158

Figures

1
Comparison of Satisfiers and Dissatisfiers   73

2
Adjustment Continua   87

3
Comparison of Satisfiers and Dissatisfiers:
Pittsburgh Engineers   97

4
Comparison of Satisfiers and Dissatisfiers:
Pittsburgh Accountants   98

5
Comparison of Satisfiers and Dissatisfiers:
Lower-Level Supervisors in Utility Industry   100

6
Comparison of Satisfiers and Dissatisfiers:
Finnish Supervisors   102

7
Comparison of Satisfiers and Dissatisfiers:
Women in High-Level Professional Positions   104

8
Comparison of Satisfiers and Dissatisfiers:
County Agriculture Extension Workers   106

9
Comparison of Satisfiers and Dissatisfiers:
Pre-Retirees from Managerial Positions   108

10
Comparison of Satisfiers and Dissatisfiers:
Scientists   110

11
Comparison of Satisfiers and Dissatisfiers:
Engineers   111

12
Comparison of Satisfiers and Dissatisfiers:
Manufacturing Supervisors   112

13
Comparison of Satisfiers and Dissatisfiers:
Male Hourly Technicians   113

14
Comparison of Satisfiers and Dissatisfiers:
Female Assemblers   114

15
Comparison of Satisfiers and Dissatisfiers:
Hospital Nurses   116

16
Comparison of Satisfiers and Dissatisfiers:
Skilled Hospital Employees   117

17
Comparison of Satisfiers and Dissatisfiers:
Unskilled Hospital Employees   118

18
Comparison of Satisfiers and Dissatisfiers:
Housekeeping Workers   119

19
Comparison of Satisfiers and Dissatisfiers:
Hungarian Engineers   121

20
Attitudes Toward Tasks   162

21
Performance Index   163

1

Business—Dominant Institution of Modern Times

ADMIRAL GEORGE W. ANDERSON, Ambassador to Portugal during the Kennedy Administration, was appointed to that position as what appeared to be a consolation prize for losing his reappointment as Chief of Naval Operations. In a speech to the National Press Club, Admiral Anderson confirmed in many minds what had been surmised—that his release from military service had been prompted by his basic disagreement with the civilian branches of the military establishment.

In the speech to the Press Club, Anderson made it clear that he was not in opposition to civilian control of the Navy, but rather to the criteria of decision making, which he felt had swung too far from the professional advice of the naval career men. Anderson implied that the business staff of the Armed Services too often outvoted the military when it came to policy determinations.

The illustration is used to introduce the proposition of the sweeping effect that the business enterprise has on all phases of life. That is, that the business organization has given its coloration, methods, skills, objectives and values to all the other institutions that serve Western societies.

Another celebrated example from the military was Charles E. Wilson's defense slogan of a "bigger bang for a buck." To some observers this turned out to have emphasized the buck, and the bang fizzled as a businessman's noise. Mr. Wilson's comments regarding the value of basic research, for instance, were in line with the way in which most modern business organizations would view truly basic research. Mr. Wilson's deprecation of such research is reflected in his statement about the foolishness of searching for what made the grass green or why fried eggs turn brown. While I wish to emphasize that I am not evaluating the merits or demerits of the business ethos, I do wish to stress the dominance of the business organization in our culture.

In my estimation, the skills and objectives of industrial managers are becoming far and away more important to our defense establishment than the skills and objectives of the West Point graduates. We are aware that the contest with the Russians is more often a tournament of relative economic and managerial strengths than a direct challenge of opposing military machines. How much defense the United States and Russia can afford depends on the economics of the problem and how efficiently each country can organize and manage its weaponry, logistics, personnel, supply and strategy. It is not too bizarre a prediction to make that one day the kind of courses now offered at the Harvard Business School may replace the curricula that the military academies are furnishing the future generals and admirals of the U.S. Armed Forces.

Closer to me, as a college professor, has been the intrusion of the business ethos into the university setting. The president of a university is spending less and less of his time as an educational leader. In many instances, the president comes from a background far from the educational arena. In addition to his obvious and historic role as a fund raiser, the college president must administer as complex an industrial organization as exists today. The head of a college is in the business of retailing education, a very "hot" item by contemporary standards, to a society that feels that education is a right—practically the fifth freedom. This right to an education has come to mean that schooling should be offered to the consumer at discount rates. To sell education at a discount requires that certain frills be eliminated. In the case of the university, two of the frills appear to be teaching and intellectual respectability. To emphasize the point that education has become merely another commodity, consider that while the tuition cost for four years of instruction at many first-rate colleges is still less than the expense of a medium-priced automobile, the increased earning power that a college degree almost guarantees makes higher education one of the most remunerative investments on the market.

Assisting the president and replacing the academic deans in influence is a new crop of vice-presidents in charge of finance, administration, fund raising, public relations, research and similar functions borrowed from the business world. More and more, the departmental chairmen, once chosen because of their distinguished scholarship, are now being chosen for managerial talents —to the mutual convenience but often to the distinct irritation of both the administration and the scholar. In addition to facing a vast increase in routine administrative duties, the chairman is concerned with financing his department by soliciting equipment, research money and training grants from the many private and governmental agencies that make up the difference in the costs of operations, because direct tuition pays only a fractional share. The chairman is also busy representing and relating his department to the growing number of other units of an increasingly complex university organization.

The business look has extended even to the individual professor, who now has his own administrative and managerial duties arising mostly from the increase and complexity of research. The professor too must raise money, supervise and administer a staff, keep books and fill out forms. In many cases, he offsets his own salary limitations by allocating increasingly large portions of his university schedule to the pursuit of grants, and often this has led to evaluation for promotion on the basis of the professor's "grantsmanship." What more businesslike criteria of success could the university adopt than those of earnings and managerial skill? Yet to the university hierarchy these qualities are becoming more important than teaching and research.

Senator Abraham Ribicoff recently commented caustically on the absence of the professor from his classroom because of the government's support of academic research. The professorial tycoon has indeed superseded the scholarly professor. Art Buchwald attributes the restlessness of the students on campus to the fact that the professor is too busy to be reached.

At the other end of the echelon is the board of trustees, which is heavily staffed with businessmen who cannot escape their own orientation and which thus confirms the concept of a university as a business not much different from any other represented by the chamber of commerce. The university has changed. Perhaps the professor and his remembered institution are part of the romantic past, for he is no longer "a scholar in a community of scholars" but an employee of a large quasi-business organization merchandising (with the appropriate cultural noises) technology, and he is seeking fringe benefits just as avidly as his nonprofessorial counterpart in industry proper.

Of late, ministers have complained that they would have been better off with a master of business administration degree instead of the traditional degree in religion. The National Council of Churches has accordingly established an executive development program at the American University in Washington, D.C., to give managerial training to its top-level people. This is identical to the executive development programs in industry. There is little doubt that a job analysis of a cleric's activities would verify the candid recognition of what the clerical role has become. In the same manner that industry has been forced to diversify its products, so has the church diversified its services. Accordingly, administrative and managerial duties have been enlarged to match the new job requirements of church employees (i.e., rabbis, ministers and priests). In some urban areas, Madison Avenue advertising techniques have been adopted to sell the idea of going to church.

But more important than all this is the role that the church has been playing as an arm of the social protrusions of industry. One of the more unseemly aspects is the continuing discrimination against Jews in line management positions that is often excused by the lame explanation that they would not fit into the church-centered social life that frequently goes on in smaller communities and in suburbs. It is as if the church were a social organization much like the country club. Membership in, or at least acceptance by, these "nonbusiness" organizations is frequently considered necessary for success in certain executive positions, particularly in the sales organization.

The University of Michigan Institute for Social Research, Survey Research Center, conducted a study for the American Jewish Committee (1964) entitled *Discrimination without Prejudice*.

This report indicates that: "The use of a worker's religion as a criterion of his promotability is not an isolated occurrence. Instead, it is seen by supervisors as occurring mainly within a promotional process which also acknowledges the importance of a worker's social background and his present social connections. If a company is seen as being attentive to a worker's religion, it is likely to be seen also as paying attention to his club, lodge, college, and other social characteristics."

Apparently, the theologian and the practicing religious clergy are becoming more subservient to the administrative and managerial hierarchy, both on the ecclesiastical and on the lay side. This separation is somewhat like the situation just described for the university, where the professor has become, more or less, the employee of the academic administrator. This complaint is usually thought of as belonging to industry, where the technical and professional staffs feel limited in their growth opportunities by their exclusion from advancement in the managerial structure. For an engineer to be a manager too often means giving up engineering; and in the same manner the professor must give up his specialty and the clergyman his preaching and ministering. Neither the university nor the church, as evidenced by the collegial authority of church administration proposed in the recent Vatican Council, feels it can adequately market its services unless it gives priority to the mechanics of the organization. The tested and proven mechanics of the business enterprise have shown their superiority and, therefore, the business methodology is adopted.

President Johnson has requested that the national government provide some sponsorship of the arts so that artists in America may direct their energies more to the aesthetic excellence of their profession than to its economics. This request is another instance of the intrusion of the business philosophy into the noneconomic institutions whose sole concern should be the intellectual and emotional needs of the people.

Perhaps the most significant of the intrusions into aesthetics for workers, though the least recognized by the general public, has taken place in the field of architecture. In the main, modern business architecture represents engineering skill used to provide the most *efficient* work space, which matches the job requirements rather than the needs of people who are working. The architect and the decorator succeed too well in constantly reminding the employee that he is a function first and foremost, indistinguishable from other similar functions in the company. In a workshop on the simplification of dental procedures, given at Western Reserve University in 1959, Philmore Hart, a practicing architect, said "the environment created for the human endeavor within the building is the function: the creation of the atmosphere of the environment is the function of the Architect." This seems to mean that the human endeavor is a function, for which space must be correctly utilized. There is more reason in this concept of architecture than in any attempt to economize in building costs. There is the intent to place human beings in settings that re-emphasize their role as a functioning part of the company as surely as the assembly line emphasizes the repertory of behavior that is permissible for factory hands.

Unfortunately, a similar concept of design has been used for residential architecture and decoration, as though living in a house were simply a problem of efficiency. Whatever decorative features still remain in building are aimed at the consumer of products or services of the company that is involved. We have been highly critical of Soviet architecture for its utilitarianism and its dedication to serving the state's philosophy, but in our convenient evasion of reality we fail to see the same process in our own building.

The performing arts are notorious for their dominant commercial goals and methods. Even the so-called arty and public-service television shows are programmed to commercial art tastes, because the business approach cannot be readily washed out of the sponsors' and creators' conscious or subconscious thoughts, although a deliberate and honest attempt to do so may be made. Witness the foreign cinema imports, which began as true expressions of artistic creativity but eventually succumbed to the hard test of business pragmatics, so that creative expression in foreign films is fast becoming only slightly more than veneer deep. Artistic criticism becomes caught up in the swirl of a breakthrough that causes it quickly to lose its distinction through commercialism. The legitimate theatre, and also music, ballet and the graphic arts, have all fallen victim to the confusion arising from the current intrusion of business into the area of new ideas and experimentation. The critic is soon victimized by this subtle alteration of the artistic product, and his ability becomes dulled when he is asked to distinguish between realism and pornography, originality and peculiarity, new dimensions and trickery. A cynical sense is inappropriate for art appreciation, but the union of art and business breeds just such a sense for self-protection.

Finally, there is one more segment of life which, above all others, has become captive to the industrial way of life—our leisure. Efficiently organized and managed, leisure has confirmed, as nothing else has, the infiltration of the business philosophy. A vacation abroad certainly demonstrates that you are engaging in leisure in large measure for, and in a manner that serves, the American Express Company and its numerous competitors. The same efficiency that organizes the "twenty-one day tour of fifteen exciting countries" also bleaches out the novelty and appreciation of discovering new experiences which are the traveler's right. By the rigid and regulated discipline of the conducted tour, the voyager is made a passive onlooker rather than an active participant, his right to explore having been taken from him. This maximizes the efficiency of the tour by minimizing the chance occurrence that is often so charming in its unexpectedness. This minimal criteria for the enjoyment of leisure approximate the philosophy that applies to assembly-line production. The principle of minimizing error by maximizing the loss of human enjoyment will be discussed in a later chapter.

Hobbies and avocations are also vitiated in their leisure benefits by the control that business organizations have taken of them in their penchant for organization and profit. Much has been said of organized and made-easy participation in various recreational activities; it has become an old story, but the trend still persists and is, in fact, going strong. Books of the month are now joined by condensed books of the month, great art pictures of the month and gifts from faraway places of the month. Even in such hallowed pastimes as scouting and Little League baseball the fun is often overshadowed by the business and organizational aspects.

These developments have been described in greater detail and with greater social criticism by others. I wish only to present a few examples of the business mentality as it has affected the various institutions that cater to man's needs, in order to suggest how it pervades our lives. This is not a new story; I think it began hundreds of years ago, when industry started its rise to dominance over all human institutions.

Not only have the systems of the businessman given their complexion to the nonbusiness institution but they have also, in fact, taken over many of its functions, as all dominant institutions eventually do. Perhaps this other side of the coin has even greater implications than the side just described so briefly.

One of the interesting incongruities of the social scene in America today is the business community's decrying the welfare state that it fears is being imposed by the government. The truth is that industry itself has entered the welfare area with a vengeance. If welfarism is supposed to destroy the individual's responsibility to provide himself and his family with security and the appurtenances of a good life, then surely industry is much more the culprit than the government.

The government can scarcely compete with the fringe benefits that so many of the corporations provide their employees. These benefits do not serve as an incentive to superior performance, but are offered more in the traditional sense of welfarism, that is, to underwrite all of man's needs. Thus the corporation, rather than the state, becomes the father upon which the employee is dependent. The change in father figure, however, makes for little change in the psychological nature of the dependency.

An excellent example of this reversal of roles is seen in that prime target of the antiwelfarist, the social security system. Under government sponsorship, social security requires the contribution of the employee as well as the employer; in contrast, retirement plans sponsored by industry are most often of the nonvested kind.

The social security system in no way restricts the individual's maneuverability or freedom to change his place of employment, while company pension plans tend to have the vicious consequence of embedding the employee in a company in which he is no longer able to maximize his potentiality. Which is more restrictive of individual freedom?

Medical-care programs are another target of the "conservatives." Under government sponsorship these programs generally are limited to Armed Forces personnel, indigent persons and the elderly, while industry frequently offers free medical care and/or free medical insurance coverage to all its employees. Government lunch programs are limited to needy children, in contrast to the free meals given by some companies and to the underwriting of the employee's cafeteria, which is a practice of most companies. Free life insurance, house subsidies, low-interest loans, educational benefits, discount purchasing, moving expenses, maternity benefits, clubs for retirees, sick pay and recreational facilities are but a few of the growing number and variety of welfare efforts on the part of industry.

The former vice-president for industrial relations of a chain of restaurants advertised, in a large metropolitan newspaper, his intention to stay awake nights thinking of more benefits for the employees of his company. He announced in the same ad that the company had purchased an out-of-town estate for the recreational enjoyment of the employees. Does this not have the sound of cradle-to-grave maintenance?

In the preface, it was mentioned that this essay emerged from participation in programs of management development. These programs have had an astonishing rate of growth, which in one sense casts aspersions on American universities for having failed in so many areas of the manager's formal education. However, education and training have been a major function of industry for a long time now, and with the rapid changes taking place in technology they will continue to play a role to an even greater degree. In truth, industry is becoming involved in education in as big a way as our formal institutions of education. The *Wall Street Journal* has described this development in industry many times. In the issue of February 2, 1965, George Melloan writes that at International Business Machines "a college graduate becoming a systems engineer spends 33 weeks out of his first five years in IBM classrooms. Few firms can match IBM's 1,800 man training staff which is said to give 10 million hours of instruction a year to employees of IBM."

As we come to practice the belief that education is a lifetime process—as this belief has found reality in the rapid pace of change—perhaps industry will have as large a commitment to education as the public school system itself. In addition to the traditional emphasis on intramural education and training (the distinction between education and training is rapidly disappearing with the increase of specialization of all jobs), industry is now heavily committed as a sponsor of formal education outside the company. One of the recruitment devices often used to lure promising college graduates to a specific company is the opportunity to return to school for advanced degrees. Education, long the responsiblility of the government and religious institutions, is rapidly becoming another responsibility of business enterprise.

Certainly, political affiliation and voting preferences are influenced more by occupational role than by any other variable. Management is awakening to this fact and is considering establishing formal means of competition with the political action arms of labor organizations by organizing its own political action counterparts.

Admiral Ben Moreell, former chairman of the board of the Jones and Laughlin Steel Company, indicated his belief that religion should play a part in the industrial complex. In an article entitled "Businessmen on Their Knees," by Duncan Norton-Taylor (*Fortune*, October, 1953), the Admiral spoke of the necessity of bringing ethics and religious precepts into all business dealings. Another sign that industry recognizes a responsibility to raise the moral tone of society was the free distribution of the inspirational magazine *Guideposts*, edited by the Reverend Norman Vincent Peale, to U.S. Steel employees.

Lastly, company-sponsored recreational programs and social functions offer another illustration of the ubiquitous role that industry plays in all segments of life today. The company town has lost its close proximity to the factory. Now employees may live in various locations and in all directions from their place of work, but still may be involved in the company just as much as if they lived in a physically circumscribed and dominated company town.

All in all, the permeation of life by the industrial spirit justifies the idea that business is the dominant institution in present-day society. Proceeding from this assumption, then, it seems appropriate to consider present myths about the nature of man and to see how the industrial monolith shapes these myths to serve its own needs. A review of earlier myths about human nature may help to clarify and bolster the thesis that myths about human psychology have always been used by the power structure in society to enable it to satisfy man's need for unifying concepts. For by fulfilling the desire for answers to the question of the purpose of existence, institutions gain and hold control of the people.

It is important to reiterate that these comments are only an effort to demonstrate the rule of the business institution over all present organizations in Western society. The issue is not whether the control of society by business is good or bad for mankind. The important issue is this: will the dominant institution take leadership in advancing the many areas it influences? Historically, when the dominant institution fails to assume leadership in its multitudinous relationships, it eventually brings about its own destruction and, in the process, does immense harm to mankind.

2

Adam and Abraham

WHILE THE RESULTS of the study *The Motivation to Work* were being presented to management for training purposes, and during the course of participation in action programs to implement the concepts derived from the book, a theory was developed concerning the two-dimensional-need system of man that had wider applications than originally intended. In that early study it was proposed that man has two sets of basic needs—his animal needs, which relate to the environment, and his distinctive human needs, which relate to the tasks with which he is uniquely involved.

This essay will seek to define a human being in terms compatible with modern industry. In the past, the accepted conceptions of man have been utilized by the dominant organizations to acquire and maintain control over society. But those organizations invariably failed to realize that those conceptions become dangerous to the social structure (and eventually to themselves) when they are no longer acceptable to the society as embodying truth.

A brief historical review of some of the prevailing ideas about the nature of man seems to indicate that dominant societal bodies have capitalized, in an opportunistic manner, on convenient definitions of human nature in order to serve their organizational needs. The validity of this point can be illustrated by an analysis of man and his institutions in the unfolding drama of history. In emphasizing the duality of man's nature, that is, the coexistence of his uniquely human needs as well as his animal needs, I wish to illustrate how the animality of man has been exploited by the hegemonic forces in society. Finally, I hope to suggest that man must rebel against the continued partial utilization of his ability, thus compelling the leaders of our society to re-evalute their notions of human nature.

A premise of this essay is that every society has to establish myths in order to sustain its institutional forms. These myths become societal canons that are willingly accepted even though patently misleading. One of the reasons they are necessary and accepted is that man has a basic need to fill in the gaps in his understanding of his universe, and in particular man seeks to understand his place in the order of life. Man's dedication to a myth system stems not only from intellectual needs but also, and perhaps more important, from the emotional support that the myth provides in unifying the great number of bewildering encounters that he must face during his life.

The need to synthesize psychological input is as important to man as is the need of the centipede to unify the action of all of his legs in order to walk. Man will disintegrate psychologically if he is unable to cope with the tremendous amount of information that he receives and if there is no possibility of giving the data some unified meaning. As man develops his ability to relate the myriad facts of experience to one another, an awareness of the unifying mechanism gives him a sense that he exists as a single, oriented individual.

Although man has often decided arbitrarily that natural law does provide satisfactory answers to the problem of unity, myth systems are much more adaptable for unification purposes than natural laws. Natural law has to be discovered; a myth has only to be created. Nature does not exist to meet man's needs and is not reliable as a cohesive power.

Of all the myths of mankind, the most far-reaching, ubiquitous and serviceable are those that deal with human nature. Since man is the indivisible unit of society, no society can exist without an implicit conception of what people are like.

The human species is the most adaptable of all living organisms, and as such, still can survive biologically while manifesting the widest, and indeed, the most bizarre patterns of behavior. As a consequence, normal responses of people are found, according to our social scientists, only within a cultural and psychological context. One society's ideal is considered by another society to be deviant behavior—an essential difference between cultures, then, is which abnormality they choose to call normal.

The definition of man lies within the loose, vertical cultural and psychological guidelines of societies; and it is confined horizontally only by narrow biological limits. All of us are free to define others in terms suitable to ourselves. The institutions of society are also free to evolve their own table of contents of human nature, which is, by the same token, a projection of institutional needs.

The dominant societal power, whether it be religious, political or economic, propounds and directs self-serving myths because of its awareness that the stronger the belief in myths the easier it is to shape human behavior. The controlling force in the culture realistically underwrites only those needs of human nature that will also serve its purposes.

It is one of the principal theses of this essay that while the most important definition of human nature comes from the institution that stands at the apex of societal control, the institutional definition of human nature is ultimately incomplete and wrong, for it is based on other than human needs.

The primary objective of the controlling organization is to maintain its own value. Thus, any attack on the myth systems that it proposes is not merely an attack on the institution's products and services but a frontal attack on the institution itself.

Institutions will perish without myths that are favorable to a climate of growth. When the myth system no longer serves a human need, a conflict results between the individual and the organization that has been using the myth system to advance its own goals. Needing the myth for its own integrity, the organization is usually unwilling to abandon the myth even when the myth becomes functionally autonomous with regard to the purpose for which it was originally created: to serve man's cognitive and emotional needs. The most important myth system that institutions have a vested interest in are the myths of human nature.

It seems appropriate to begin with a very early definition of man and his nature as delineated in the Bible.

As Freud said, in *Moses and Monotheism*: "When I use Biblical tradition here in such an autocratic and arbitrary way, draw on it for confirmation, and dismiss its evidence without scruple when it contradicts my conclusions, I know full well that I am exposing myself to severe criticism concerning my method and that I weaken the force of my proofs." However, I will risk the criticism in order to make what I think is a worthwhile point.

In the Old Testament, there are two significant versions of the nature of man. There are, of course, many other commentaries describing the human condition, but these two are described as proceeding directly from God. One concept is in His creation of Adam and the other in His covenant with Abraham and Moses.

The first definition of man is in the creation of Adam. Adam was created as the perfect man, albeit "feeble-minded" because he was created without knowledge. "And the Lord God commanded the man, saying 'Of every tree of the garden thou mayest eat, but of the tree of knowledge of good and evil, thou shalt not eat of it; for in the day that thou eatest thereof thou shalt surely die.'" (Genesis 2:16.)

Rashi, the great Biblical commentator of the eleventh century, had this to say about the assumption that man was feeble-minded before he ate from the tree of knowledge. In explanation of the passage, "and the eyes of both them were unclosed," in reference to their having eaten from the tree, Rashi believed that the eye relates not to sight, but to the mind's eye or intelligence. Further corroboration can be had from the latter part of the same sentence, "and they knew they were naked," because, Rashi says, even a blind person knows when he is naked. Thus, by implication, Adam must have been feeble-minded before partaking of the fruit of the tree of knowledge.

We know that, according to the Biblical tradition, when Adam ate of the fruit of the tree of knowledge, God cast him out of Eden. This action by God has been interpreted as man's life sentence to suffer; for others, it is the moment when man came into his own potentiality—to fly with his own wings rather than remain completely dependent on God's Will, in the manner of a puppet manipulated by the puppeteer.

Two millennia of teaching have convinced many men that when Adam was cast out of the Garden, mankind was doomed, warped and bound to a lifetime of pain. This notion of man's sinfulness conceives of the whole purpose of existence as a sentence of suffering for Adam's fall. Therefore, man's overriding need is to avoid the multitude of pain-provoking events that are found in his new alienated environment, outside the gates of Paradise. But man in this condition is akin to all animals, and his basic motivation is thus the avoidance of pain. The function of this myth, then, is to give meaning to the meaningless; positive form to the amorphous pain of life.

The other view of man's nature first appeared in the conversation between God and Abraham: "And when Abram was ninety years old and nine, the Lord appeared to Abram, and said unto him; I am God Almighty; walk before Me, and be thou wholehearted, and I will make My covenant between Me and thee and will multiply thee exceedingly. . . . And thou shalt be the father of a multitude of nations." (Genesis 17:1.)

The second definition of man, as epitomized in Abraham, can be interpreted as meaning that man is capable, that he had been given innate potential, indeed, so much potential that God has chosen him to be His emissary on earth. In addition, by God's gift of the Ten Commandments to Moses and his followers, man came to know God by translating his God-given attributes into ethics and laws to govern human behavior.

Man created in the image of God—why is this important to the thesis of this essay? We can only guess at the peculiar circumstances that led to this singular cohesion of the definition of man's relationship to God with the Judaic definition of human nature. If man should have the potential of ample achievement and of exalted fulfillment—as the Jews believed—then man has to partake of Godlike qualities to be made in His image.

The idea that man was created in the image of God was evidence to the Jews that men were capable of great accomplishments because they were given divine abilities. It seems compatible with the thesis of this essay to point out that the hieratic order found it necessary to develop other concepts of human nature in order to provide additional answers that would give value and meaning to life. The priesthood, by rounding out and enlarging upon the myths, managed to keep the leadership of the tribes in its hands.

Here in the Bible is the history of a people bursting the bonds of slavery and setting forth into the unknown. The subsequent trials they were to face challenged Moses to the limits of his ability. As leader of the Hebrews, Moses had to shape his organizational needs to make full use of the desires of his followers. The genius that was Moses', as is true of any great leader, was that he understood the unconscious motives of his people and was able to generate a series of myths with which to control the responses of his supporters whenever the circumstances demanded. The question is, what was the essential need and what was the essential quality that emerged?

Slaves who cast off the condition of slavery require some hopeful future, some meaning to give unity to their lives. During the Exodus, the all-encompassing need of the Jewish people was a sense of tribal destiny. Clearly, the Jews, wandering in the wilderness, had to aspire to goals that were different from those of established societies of the ancient world. The Jews were too few in number to strive to build great cities and other secular monuments that would reflect the glory of their kingdom on earth. So the landless Jews projected most of their aspirations in terms of the spiritual rather than the material world. They aspired to greatness by the development of their intellectual and ethical potentialities.

When Moses talked in terms of the enormous achievements the Jews could attain by fulfilling God's design, he supplied answers to the needs of the Jews—the need to apply a unifying concept to their lives. The force, the impetus, the driving spirit, the ethos of a people, was focused on the Jewish struggle for greatness in terms of the development of the highest form of human capability. The combination of spirit and intellect had fused and presaged the main part of the Jewish contribution to Western civilization.

When the Jews triumphed in Canaan, suggesting (according to the Mosaic belief) that man was capable of achieving God's ends, the Jewish state reverted to a condition similar to that of any other political community. In this process the old Mosaic definition of man's capability floundered as the inevitable corruption of human nature caused by the rising competitive society took place.

In the words of the prophet Isaiah on the disintegration of the Jewish nation: "How is the faithful city become an harlot! It was full of judgment; righteousness lodged in it; but now murderers. Thy silver is become dross, thy wine mixed with water. Thy princes are rebellious, and companions of thieves, everyone loveth gifts, and followeth after rewards: they judge not the fatherless, neither doth the cause of the widow come unto them." (Isaiah 1:21.)

As a reaction, some Jews created ascetic movements, and perhaps the best documented was the group known as the Essenes. The Essenes put all their trust in man's direct relationship to God, rather than place any dependence upon the Mosaic concept of man's inherent worth. The complete trust in God's revealed power developed into a new theology: a theology that led to a revised Messianic concept. Its newness centered upon the God that was made man, and now fulfillment of the law was not the epitome of human efforts, but rather man was fulfilled through a Messiah who would intercede to redeem the sin of Adam.

Whether the Essenes' view of human nature became influential enough to pervade much intellectual thought beyond their sect at the time is still not known, but the view of human nature that the Essenes held reappeared so strongly in early Christian theology that it is believed possible that Jesus of Nazareth came in contact with their teachings. There was no heaven or hell in Jewish theology. Man came to know and love God through the Law, and in so doing became fully man. When he died, he lived only in the memories of those who knew him to be a good Jew and in the seed of Abraham, which he had passed on to his children. Christ promised man an eternal life of Paradise in Heaven with God. The early Christians believed that the Second Coming of Christ was imminent and that all who were worthy would be redeemed. Thus, the change in the idea of life's purpose emerged. Man had two forms of existence: one, his earthly body and its life; the other, his eternal soul. The salvation of man's soul was now the objective rather than the goal of man's human endeavor, which was an expression of God's design in His covenant with Abraham and Moses.

But the Christians had, in turn, to face up to the failure of their expectations of a Second Coming of Christ. By the fourth century, the followers of Christ realized that a re-evaluation was necessary. Rather than being charged solely with the preparation for salvation, the Church now became the custodian of a complex theology that was to provide sanctions for current behavior as well as for future goals. By means of this evaluation, the Church became the dominant institution in society, and soon it was no longer centered only on the problem of imminent salvation but also became important to the maintenance of the organizational needs of the Church itself.

It has been said that a great part of the heresy controversies and the episcopacy movement did not consist of quarrels about the question of the Second Coming, but focused instead on the integrity of the Christian community and the nature of the Church itself. Therefore, the Church became an organic structure in society, competing with the secular powers and endeavoring to serve man's desire for unity of experience.

This led to a conflict between the political institution in power, the Roman Empire, and the dominant religious force, the Roman Church. Until the reign of Constantine, Roman emperors had viewed all religious practices benignly. In fact, the rulers drew strength from this tolerance, believing that religion would serve to unify the state. Thus all religious systems were tolerated by the Roman government.

When Christianity became a useful political tool, the Emperor Constantine was quick to take advantage of the small but well-disciplined group of Roman subjects. Ferdinand Lot, the French medievalist, says that historians are not sure that Constantine ever actually became a convert to Christianity. According to Lot, "apart from the Christian apologists, historians agree in seeing the founder of the Christian Empire as a shrewd statesman, at bottom a religious sceptic or at the most, a deist."

At this time in history, the needs of men for a new unification of experience and the needs of the dominant organization to maintain its position of leadership came into juxtaposition. In what ways did the doctrines of the Catholic Church unify human experience? The Church stated that man was sinful, but promised salvation to all who would sincerely repent of their sins. In turn, the state made use of the Christian definition of human nature by asserting that the natural depravity of man made additional safeguards of a legal system necessary for his control as well. This was the initial use of the Christian theology as a myth system by a state, wherein both Church and state utilized the identical definition of human nature to serve their separate purposes.

The Middle Ages saw the Church emerge victorious in the struggle for ascendancy in society. By the eleventh century, according to the medievalist Frederick Artz, "the papacy found itself able to direct the whole of Western society. The church attempted to unify all life, politically, economically and most important to control the life of the individual and of the family, through the sacramental sense." This is not much different from the description of business as the dominant institution of our present society.

One of the foremost spokesman for the Church in the thirteenth century was Thomas Aquinas. In his great work, the *Summa Theologica*, he discusses his views on human nature. He says he does not believe that human happiness consists in values of the body because it cannot "be that the main goal of a thing if used as a means for something else should be to protect its own existence." Aquinas uses the example of the ship, whose main purpose is to carry cargo, not merely to be seaworthy. Besides, Aquinas goes on to say, even if one conceded that the aim of human reason and will is the survival of the human self, one cannot say that the goal of man is a value of the body. For Aquinas concludes that the goals of man are "neither outside or within him, they transcend him."

Apparently the Angelic Doctor is denying man's ability to achieve the goal of absolute happiness, because when Aquinas defines man as incapable of providing his own solutions to the problem of salvation, it seems implicit in the argument that there is no need for man to seek solutions. In effect, man's inherent ability to realize his potential solely by his own efforts seemed to be denied him.

Despite the dominance of the Church as an institution in the late medieval period, other forces emerged, and a mighty struggle took place as the Roman Church sought to maintain its control over all aspects of life. As all organizations increase their control and dominance in society, they must match this control with an ever-increasing dedication to propounding the myths concerning human nature that best serve the interests of the organization. The Church, whose prime function had been the salvation of souls, now found it necessary to augment its role. The Church did this by emphasizing the depravity of man, which increased the need for the Church to take more leadership in the temporal world. The view of mankind that was held by the Church was too painful for men to bear. In *Mont-Saint-Michel and Chartres,* Henry Adams says, "In that law, no human weakness or error could exist; by its essence it was infinite, eternal, immutable. There was no crack in the system through which human frailty could hope for escape."

That man cannot live without hope of positive human attributes seems further amplified by the appearance of the cult of Mariolatry. The medieval Church had denied man the chance to participate in his own salvation. The Day of Judgment and the terrible justice that awaited were too awful to face. In desperation, the people turned to Mary and prayed for her intercession.

The Adam view of human nature was losing its importance as a unifying concept. H. J. Muller regards the Virgin as "the most vital religious symbol for millions of simple worshippers, for whom the Trinity is much too remote and abstract, and God himself is too awful." The value of the Christian myth system was decreasing.

Worshipping Mary became a means of elevating the conception of human nature to include positive assets as well as the denigrated characteristics that embodied the conception of man held by the Church. If, in the eyes of His believers, Christ has become such a foreboding and vindictive image, then perhaps Mary, as a mother, might see some good in even the worst child. An alien spirit emerged from the conflict between the Church and its supporters, heralding, as Henry Adams said, "the termination of the unity of Church and State, God and man, and life and death."

The fourteenth century saw the criticism of the Church on a number of fronts. The seizing of the Papacy and its removal to

Avignon by Philip of France were another indication that the power of the Church as the leader in the affairs of the temporal and secular world was weakening. Toward the middle of the century, the Hundred Years' War turned men from contemplation of the future of the soul to the current problems of physical survival.

The fifteenth century witnessed the firm entrenchment of the monarchy—absolute in France, restricted in England. Everywhere, the middle class was beginning to defy religious and state authorities. Almost imperceptibly, Italian society became secularized. What is important is the change that was wrought upon the definition of human nature by the intense interest in the secular world. This does not mean that everyone was in opposition to the philosophy of the Church or the Christian religion. But man was in revolt against the idea that it was sinful to obtain satisfaction from human achievements. Renaissance man felt that human accomplishments were worth while when they gave men pleasure, which was yet another manifestation of God's will, as essential to man's well-being as was the need for salvation.

The medieval view that man was controlled by his animality was no longer the dominant view held by society. The Renaissance awakened the belief that achievement was an important need for mankind. The thesis that achievement is as necessary to the happiness of mankind as is the gratification of man's animal needs was rekindled in the spirit of the Renaissance.

Pico della Mirandola, in his *Oration on the Dignity of Man*, remarks on the falseness of the view that man owes his uniqueness in the universe to his position in the center of it. Man's real power lies in his ability to choose what value his life should have. "To him it is granted to have whatever he chooses, to be whatever he will."

However, the conflict between the individual and the establishment was important in terms of man's psychological development, because it endured from the beginning of the Christian era until the end of the fourteenth century. Biology suggests that interference in the early stages of development has the most profound effects on the potentiality of the organism. The Middle Ages and the proto-Renaissance, as stages in modern man's psychological development, served to perpetuate the concept of the natural depravity of man—the Adam view of human nature. By analogy, the Renaissance was a genuine rebirth of man's need to achieve, a return to the conception of the Abraham view of mankind.

The decisive blow to the unity of the Christian world came with the Protestant Reformation. The Renaissance had channeled interest from heaven to earth, while at the same time a rising nationalism dealt a deathblow to the political unity of Europe and devitalized the power of the Papacy. The Protestant Revolt not only rent Europe but also spawned institutions that were in competition with the Church.

The return to the stern God of the Old Testament that found expression in Calvin's view of human nature is germane to this essay because it had an overwhelming influence on the contemporary concept of human nature. The basis of Calvin's theology was his belief that man was completely worthless because he had inherited Adam's sin. Man can be saved, according to Calvin, only by the grace of God. Calvin maintained that God in eternity had said that there would be the fall of man in Adam and that God would then elect some of the damned for salvation. The knotty theological problem that resulted in the doctrine of the Elect was solved by the Calvinists when they said that men would know intuitively whether they were to be saved or damned. In addition, Calvinists believed that the Elect *must participate in the affairs of this world,* thereby putting forward the concept of work as a vocation in which men served God.

Economic success came to be looked upon as evidence of self-denial and sacrifice to the glory of God. The Calvinists were actively involved in the political, social and economic affairs of the seventeenth century. The Protestant Revolt can be seen as further evidence of the overriding need of the individual to express himself, but it was a paradoxical period. It was then that man saw himself on the one hand as degraded and eternally damned, and on the other hand as being only a little less than an angel and able to secure his own salvation.

Man's identification with Adam caused man to attempt to reverse the alienation from God that Adam suffered. The Reformation (in origin, a protest against the passivity of man in the affairs of the spirit) became an instrument to free man in order that he might realize his innate potential in this world.

Every revolution has caused radical revisions in the power structure of society. New myth systems are born when the old dogmas hurt people too much. A problem that the leaders of revolutionary movements must face is how to win the people away from the standards of an outdated value system and encourage them to give allegiance to a new order, an order that will better serve the current organizational needs of the revolutionary leadership.

The emergence of industry as the dominant organization in society took place, I think, as a result of the Industrial Revolution. This revolution was an inevitable consequence of the view of man as having positive potentialities, although this notion was hidden under the cloak of both the old and the new theologies.

To understand the myths of man that have been propounded and perpetuated by the industrial organization, it is necessary to examine some psychological highlights of the beginnings of the Industrial Revolution. The era of the Industrial Revolution is recognizable enough in broad outline, having taken place primarily between the eighteenth and nineteenth centuries in Europe. As a clearly delineated event or series of events, it offers little preciseness. The boundaries of ages in history are many, and they are really only useful as the tools of the historian—to enable him to focus more closely on his particular subject.

For the industrial psychologist, the period of the Industrial Revolution becomes a limited part of historical time during which there was a change in the way people looked at themselves and at others. This shift in viewpoint took place upon the advent of new dominant institutions—when the entrepreneur emerged as a controlling force in society.

Initially, the industrial development in the economy encompassed two fundamental principles: the way goods are produced and the measure of successful production. The manner in which goods were manufactured created a shift in the man-tool relationship, because the tools of man became the important member of the team and the man became the tool's helper. As the tool grew to factory proportions, the function of man was curtailed and the worker became an interchangeable specialized instrument, so that the tool took over the direction and coordination of the task.

The measure of success that was the result of this labor was not the satisfaction evidenced by the consumer or the producer but the balance of profits over losses. It was this merger of technology with capital that produced capitalism and the new leaders of society, the capitalists. The fertility of the merger is surpassed only by the begetting union of Adam and his rib.

The new technology and economic philosophy required a different role for people who produced the goods and a different conception of the value of what they produced; both ideas were relatively unique in man's experience. Labor has always been the lot of man, but his labor up to the period of the Industrial Revolution was usually dictated by the physical world and by other people. In contemporary Western culture, man is often controlled by his machines. One can praise, curse, beseech and worship Mother Nature or even other men, but machines have rarely appealed emotionally to man. There is no mystique in a machine to which a man can rationally relate—it is difficult to develop a loyalty to a punch press. Even the programmer of the modern computer machine has become a motivational problem, despite the fact that his job allows him much more freedom of action than that enjoyed by the man whose job is limited by his position on the assembly line. The high turnover and the lack of morale among computer-machine programmers have been discussed recently. This turnover seems to indicate that the initial challenge of programming computers soon turns into routine drudgery. When that happens, the machine loses its status as an instrument for the programmer's determinism, as surely as the assembly line once did for the blue-collar worker. Instead of being determined by its operator, the computer becomes, in a sense, an instrument to determine the programmer.

At the time of the Industrial Revolution there was also a change in the purpose of work. This change was brought about by the development of the capitalist idea, which alienated the worker from his conception of the value of work. When production is in the service of perceived consumption, as it was in the preindustrial society, there was little difficulty in relating the role of the worker to his work. This relationship was apparent regardless of the material benefits personally derived by the worker. Thus, a slave may be producing for others and receive little of the fruits of his labor himself, but he can easily understand the goal of his efforts—that is, work or starve. When the goal of production is simply for the color of a bookkeeper's ink, it is too great an abstraction for significant comprehension on the part of the worker. Even today, after years of modern economics, the relationship between capital and consumer needs is foreign to most people, despite their ready acceptance of this way of life.

Some time ago, I conducted a morale survey for a company and was asked by management to discuss some unfavorable results of their "freedom-education" program. The program was designed to educate the employee in the basic tenets of the capitalistic system, in the hope that greater understanding would lead to a more acceptable attitude toward management. The message involved the usual series of partially true deductions, as follows: If the worker produces more, the company can sell the product more cheaply; if the company sells the product more cheaply, it will sell more; if it sells more, it will make more profits; if profits increase, then operations can expand; if operations expand, more jobs will be created and labor will be scarcer. Now we come to the point. This method of reasoning leads to the conclusion that if labor is scarce, the worker will be worth more and *then* his work will be rewarded.

Such a system of deductive reasoning may or may not make good economic sense, but psychologically speaking it represents a vast circumlocution with a devious, tenuous and delayed reinforcement for the worker. In *Capital,* Karl Marx commented on the problem of delayed reinforcement. In discussing "capitalist production," Marx says:

> The purchase of labour-power for a fixed period is the prelude to the process of production; and this prelude is constantly repeated when the stipulated term comes to an end. . . . But the labourer is not paid until after he has expended his labour-power, and realized in commodities not only its value, but surplus value. . . . The capitalist, it is true, pays him in money, but this money is merely the transmuted form of the product of his labour.

Marx's understanding was based on an economic criticism rather than on a psychological evaluation. While the economic system of Marx has not found justification in subsequent economic results, the psychological arguments are still apparently valid. Obviously, the reinforcement is too far away from the task and the reasoning is conducted along too tortuous a path for effective persuasion. The "freedom program" engendered a feeling of suspicion among the workers, who felt that the program was another attempt on the part of management to increase production rather than to enlighten the worker as to the meaning of freedom.

In the same manner, the Industrial Revolution required many psychological alterations in the life of the people. I have reference to the drastic uprooting of the farm population and its removal to factory sites. The necessity of bringing the work population to the factory dealt a deathblow to the agrarian way of life and, at the same time, to its social system.

This relocation of the farm population carried with it the breakdown of tremendous psychological forces that had been built up in order to sustain the feudal societies. The manorial system had produced an ethos that provided the answers to the questions man continually asks himself: What is life all about? What am I doing here? The explanation afforded the individual who lived under the protection of the feudal hierarchy fulfilled man's need to live as a unity. When the psychological and social aspects are considered, it is apparent that there was stability and order in society. As Tevye philosophizes in the play *Fiddler on the Roof:* "Because of our traditions, everyone here knows who he is and what God expects him to do."

This stability could be observed in the important relationships that defined each person's obligations to others. Whatever the merits of these person-to-person connections, it was their existence that cemented the disparate elements of life. For example, in such a society there is the connection of consequence between the lord of the manor (the boss in England) and the villein, serf or peasant (the bossed).

While it was one-sided, repressive, exploitative and based on the most specious of reasoning, this relationship did contain a *quid pro quo,* a two-way contractual set of obligations of mutual aid. If the peasant owed the master his labor and his fidelity, in return the lord owed protection, security, advice and various paternalistic concerns. The important consideration is that *the total human being was implicated in these relationships.* It is essential to appreciate the psychological need of belonging that is invested in established relationships, even when the relationships contain pathological ingredients. The changeover from the rural-based, protected life to the urban industrial society was much more earth-shaking to the psychological well-being of the individual than previous shifts in allegiance had been.

The thesis that the dominant organization must shape man's needs the better to serve its own ends becomes blatantly apparent at this time in history. A new myth system was needed. In other words, a fresh characteristic spirit must capture the allegiance of the populace by providing new or different answers to serve the needs of mankind for psychological unity. But before the people can accept a new scheme, the old one must be destroyed. The problem facing the new leadership is how to tear the people away from the standards of the outdated value system and make them swear allegiance to a new order that will serve the current needs of the organization. It is possible to chip away at the old by attacking the flagrantly obsolescent parts, and then spotlighting the improvements that the new method will offer; but this is the way to gradual change, not to a revolution.

A much more fundamental operation is required if a revolt is necessary—an operation that severs the unifying factors from human existence. A solvent is necessary to separate the parts that make up a total psychological life, and in the process prepare people for a new ethos. The old universal solvent for revolution is that apogee of all man's aspirations, "Freedom."

The cry "Freedom" has been the anthem of all revolts, whether political, social, aesthetic, economic or psychological. The potency of the freedom cry stems from the sanctions it offers for discarding many relationships, obligations and encumbrances. Freedom gives promise of new beginning.

To start life over, to have another chance in this world, to have a second try—all are implied in the concept of freedom. The idea of freedom strikes to the heart of the human dream. It is a postponement of mortality—"there is still time."

The Industrial Revolution and capitalism were intertwined,

each making the other possible. In England the businessman pursued his course in an atmosphere of laissez faire. The government was sympathetic with the aims of business, often enacting legislation designed to aid businessmen, and more often simply staying out of the capitalist's way. Later, on the Continent, particularly in Germany, the government acted more as the sponsor by encouraging industrialization via cartel monopolies. The entrepreneur required loose reins on his activities so that he might move quickly in exploiting the new sources of power made available by the new technology.

Institutions and a definition of human nature rooted in a preindustrial social order were drags on the industrialist's efforts. Because the industrialist needed to be free from the state to pursue an uncharted course, it followed that all men should be free from all previous commitments to assure minimum barriers to the business enterprise. As translated to the management of labor, this means that each worker was free to seek his own development and to bargain for his services in the open market. All the old contractual obligations were void, the worker was free to work or not to work and the manager was free to hire him or not to hire him.

Furthermore, management had no obligations beyond the individual bargaining agreement, which was centered in the wage the boss paid for the labor he received. Unlike a feudal arrangement, the only relationship between the employer and the employee was the work done for specified wages. Other than that the management had no responsibility toward the worker.

The various components of a job, those that include working conditions, social responsibility for the employees and the needs of the community in general, were outside the management's purview. The result is the perennial treason of enslaving man by waving before him the banner of his most cherished need but keeping the attainment of it just out of reach.

If man was to believe in his freedom when such a belief was manifestly absurd, then some means to reduce the cognitive dissonance had become necessary. Such a naked incongruity can lead only to the feeling of psychological conflict, frustration and eventually aggression. A slave is in no psychological conflict—he has an unenviable life and he knows it; but a man suffers who thinks he is free but is psychologically enchained.

The American Negro provides a ready example to illustrate this proposition. The Negro is in deep psychological distress because every law of the land and every sacred document of American history says he is free, but obviously his freedom is expressed mainly in words, not in action.

A comprehensive summary of contradictory assumptions of American values, with each side of the contradiction held to be equally true by many Americans, was listed by Robert S. Lynd in his book *Knowledge for What?* (1939):

. . . Everyone should try to be successful.

But: The kind of person you are is more important than how successful you are.

. . . The family is our basic institution and the sacred core of our national life.

But: Business is our most important institution, and, since national welfare depends upon it, other institutions must conform to its needs.

. . . Life would not be tolerable if we did not believe in progress and know that things are getting better. We should, therefore, welcome new things.

But: The old, tried fundamentals are best; and it is a mistake for busybodies to try to change things too fast or to upset the fundamentals.

. . . Honesty is the best policy.

But: Business is business, and a businessman would be a fool if he didn't cover his hand.

. . . Education is a fine thing.

But: It is the practical men who get things done.

. . . Science is a fine thing in its place and our future depends upon it.

But: Science has no right to interfere with such things as business and our other fundamental institutions. The thing to do is to *use* science, but not let it upset things. . . .

This same kind of conflict between myth and reality was engendered by the Industrial Revolution. New myths were required to smooth over the conflict between the prevailing ethic and the facts of life: new myths were needed to replace the ancient ones that were suited only to a feudal way of life.

The concept of individual freedom succeeded in loosening the bonds that cemented together various meanings in life, but this new condition necessitated the replacement of some unifying principles by others that would serve as well.

Two such principles were available. One was the Protestant ethic and the other was social Darwinism. These two myths provided a necessary revision to the conceptions of the nature of man that had been used so long and so successfully in the past. The industrial leadership, having become the dominant force in society, used the myths of the Protestant ethic and of social Darwinism to reshape the concept of human nature that had previously been held.

A redefinition of human nature was the problem for the business organization as the new dominant institution that arose as a result of the Industrial Revolution. The achievement needs of man once more appeared to find a receptive climate, but, as it turned out, the business institution merely altered the contents of man's avoidance needs. Rather than being motivated by fear of sin, man was now defined by a set of secular counterparts.

3

Industry's Concepts of Man

IN CONTEMPORARY SOCIETY, business is the dominant institution. It is industry that has been defining the basic characteristics of the human. Some of the prevailing myths that industry has served up, primarily to justify its own "need" views regarding the nature of worker motivation and the nature of man, deserve to be carefully examined.

"Seest thou a man diligent in his business? He shall stand before Kings." (Proverbs 22:29) Or, as the Reverend M. D. Babcock said in a sermon delivered in 1900, which summarized very neatly the doctrine of the Protestant ethic: "Business is religion and religion is business. The man who does not make a business of his religion has a business life of no character. . . ."

Captains of industry were thought to be the leaders of men and nations; without their guidance, the workers would live in squalor and want. Virtue was defined as economic success, and economic success was defined as evidence of virtue. This myth about human nature is part of what has been labeled the "Protestant ethic." Reinhard Bendix, professor of sociology at the University of California, has described this thesis eloquently in his book *Work and Authority in Industry.*

The myth that was exemplified by the Protestant ethic was bred from the Calvinistic doctrine of predestination and of the "calling of the Elect."

Martin Luther's concept that the individual must be responsible for his own salvation, independent of the church's function as a mediator between him and God, was a radical departure from previous religious beliefs. John Calvin expanded this concept by suggesting that passive faith was insufficient for salvation. By adding the doctrine of predestination, Calvin augmented the belief in the omnipotence of God—that He knew not only the past and the present but also, and more important, the future. As the creed of predestination was stated in the Westminster Confession of 1647, "By the decree of God, for the manifestation of His Glory, some men and angels are predestinated unto everlasting life, and others foreordained to ever-lasting death."

In a system such as Calvin's, what tangible evidence, what manifestation on this earth, could one use to determine whether or not he is marked for salvation? The popular interpretation of predestination turned out that the chosen would be those who could measure their success in business values, and success became the sign of the "Elect."

The Industrial Revolution and the breakdown of the traditional way of life were justified by the religious ethic. God had planned it this way, according to some latter-day Puritans. The poor were the "great, dirty unwashed." Not only were they indolent and without ambition, but they were also marked for perdition. This seemed obvious for if they were of the "Elect," they would have been successful. Business had found a justification for its concept of human nature—it was God's will. The Protestant ethic was not based on Calvin's original theology. Here begins the emergence of management's myth of the "economic man."

Economic man replaced spiritual man, and the result was the scientific explosion. Contemplation of the soul was replaced by the empirical study of the body; concepts of heavenly bodies were replaced by concepts of mass and motion. The basic approach that man used in his intellectual activities changed from scholastic logic to scientific methodology. This does not mean that the impetus of this explosion was a new sanction given to economic man, but rather the rebirth of the concept of freedom given to Abraham.

The nineteenth century saw the fruition of the age of rationality. A scientific explanation was needed in addition to the religious interpretation provided by the Protestant ethic. Charles Darwin produced the scientific rationale when he published the *Origin of Species* in 1859. He suggested that only those species that were biologically fittest could survive their environment. Darwin's theories of biological evolution fell nicely into place, because the concept of the survival of the fittest in the biological jungle was enlarged to include survival in the economic jungle. Those organizations and individuals that survived competition were evidently the hardiest—they had the proper mutation for survival. It was social Darwinism, as Max Weber described it in *The Protestant Ethic and the Spirit of Capitalism.*

The Protestant ethic then developed two structures. There were the religious sanctions and there were the scientific explanations for the achievement of economic success. But, as time passed, the workers could not tolerate a system in which most of them were defined as unfit and damned and their ill treatment by management so justified. The myth system involved in this definition of man constituted a pathology that created painful reactions.

An era of social welfare was ushered in, under the cloak of humanitarianism. That was the manifest reason. Bendix holds that the fear of radicalism was the latent reason for the new humanitarian consideration of the worker. The political right in history has frequently stolen the thunder on the left by means of social legislation. The attempt to be humane developed into a philosophy of welfare capitalism or paternalism. The height of welfare capitalism in the United States parallels the greatest fears that the nation has had of radicalism, which occurred in the 1920s as an aftermath of the Russian Revolution. Management continued to adhere to its original belief in the Protestant ethic, but now it buttressed its position regarding the worker by inaugurating a social welfare program within industry.

Paternalism may be considered a first approach toward including a human relations concept of industrial relations—a motivation program. The precept that the worker has to work out of duty is no longer valid, and it becomes apparent to management that the worker must be willing—if not eager—to work. Once this principle is recognized, managers have a responsibility to do something about the motivation to work. Industry agrees to certain social legislation and management takes limited responsibility for the worker. However, this trend has developed into an overdone paternalistic concern for the worker, which ends up in welfare capitalism. An attempt is made to equate the balance of what I describe later as hygiene needs by treating the worker better, paying him more and paying him for doing the job the way management wishes it done.

Here is an additional theory of labor and of job motivation: people work effectively when they are well treated physically. It becomes the manager's responsibility to see that the worker, in addition to being paid, is comfortable; and when this happens, management believes it should follow that all of the worker's motivational drives will be elicited.

The next step necessary in developing a new myth is the formulation of the concept that the worker is a creature of physical needs. He is an economically determined man, but he is also a creature of comfort. The raw nerve of the worker may be his money motivation, but in addition there are physical and security demands he makes while at work.

Frederick Taylor, in his book *Scientific Management*, said that what the manager really ought to do is discover the best way to do the job, provide the right tools, select the right man, train him in the right way of doing the job, give him incentives if he does perform the job correctly, and by doing all of these things, he should motivate the worker to work. But the impact of Taylorism was felt not solely by the worker but by management as well. The problem of how to manage workers was to be solved not on the basis of pseudoscientific beliefs but rather on managerial know-how in utilizing human resources. Taylor did not envision that his work would result in an almost inhuman society—as catastrophic to human dignity as that protrayed by Charlie Chaplin in *Modern Times*.

On the contrary, Taylor felt that if management adopted scientific methods, worker dignity and welfare would be benefited. In a letter discussing Taylor's feelings about the hatred that both capital and labor bore him, Scudder Klyne, a naval lieutenant and Taylor's close friend, said, "It is my personal opinion from hearing Taylor talk that his sympathies are almost entirely with labor, but that he considers it more of an immediate possibility to get capital to start cooperating than it is to educate labor to it." In this view, Taylor essentially was not far wrong; the error was in estimating the intelligence of management.

If the managers lamented the fact that the worker was not doing an exceptional job and that he was complaining and was nonproductive, Taylor countered with, "You don't know how to manage." He believed also that management had no right to expect the blossoming of a devotion to duty on the part of the workers; it was up to management to utilize the work force properly.

Managers soon adopted the principles of scientific management, with its basic discipline—industrial engineering. The essence of industrial engineering as applied to people is to remove the effects of one of the prime laws of psychology, the law of individual differences. That is, if one man has ten talents, another nine, and others eight, seven, six, and on down the line to one, the most efficient procedure would be to structure and limit the work task so that the one talent held in common would be utilized. This technique provides for the elimination of variability or individual differences. In this way, the possibility of error is minimized, but the maximization of the waste of human talents also takes place. The ten, nine, eight, and so-on talents that people possess are suppressed in order to insure freedom from error. (An added return to management is a reduction in the cost of training and retraining; for if the job is simplified, then almost anyone can be brought in to do it, and this reduces the cost of absenteeism and turnover.) But as production processes change from individual units to the production of subunits in large numbers, the cost of error increases. When a small subunit is spoiled, all the larger units of which it is a part are also spoiled— not just one total assembly, as in previous assembly operations where the worker was responsible for the total unit.

This system of utilizing only the lowest common denominator in the catalogue of ability was a consequence of Taylor's theory of scientific management. Using only the minimum in a man's repertory of behavior was, in a sense, amputating the rest of his capabilities. Industrial society needed a new myth to justify this denigration of man and it created the myth of the "mechanistic man."

This new notion suggested that the overriding desire of the worker was to be utilized efficiently and with a minimum of effort. That man is happiest when he is "an interchangeable part of an interchangeable machine making interchangeable parts" has become an axiom.

People were thought to be delighted with the fact that they did not have to make decisions. Management believed that those people were happy workers who did not have the responsibilities of management. The concept of the idyllically happy worker attuned to the factory system in which all decisions were made for him was as erroneous as the Rousseauan myth of the "Noble Huron."

The emphasis of research in industrial psychology in the 1920s was related to boredom, fatigue and the efficiency of the organism as a machine. What are the best uses of the human machine? How long can it run before it breaks down and needs to be lubricated? What are the environmental conditions under which this machine will operate most efficaciously? These are the problems that prompted the Hawthorne plant of the Western Electric Company to begin what is now considered a landmark study in industrial relations. The Hawthorne Studies (1927–1932) were undertaken to probe the effects of change in the physical environment on the human machine. The researchers found no consistent correlation and no rationality between the many changes in the physical environment of the place of work and the productivity of the worker.

To the scientists, it appeared that a poltergeist was at work at Hawthorne. The physical scientists threw up their hands and walked out, suggesting that this was a problem for witch doctors, not for them; and management sent for the behavioral scientists. As there was a suspicion that ghosts were at work, the behavioral scientists were forced to resort to the most primitive method of science, observation. The scientists sat and they watched.

After years of observation, the behavioral scientists concluded that the worker was not living up to the prevailing myth system of worker motivation. He was restricting output, with the result that he was making less money. Here was a situation in which man was set up to operate most efficiently in order to improve his economic lot, but somehow he was operating inefficiently. He was denying himself the reward of more money so that his fellow workers would like him.

It seemed that to the worker the informal organization and his place in it became more important than the traditional rational reasoning—his economic gain. On the basis of these conclusions, the Western Electric Company initiated a rather sizable program of surveying morale and followed it up with an extensive employee-counseling program.

Elton Mayo, late professor of industrial research at Harvard University and one of the directors of the Hawthorne study, was a great social scientist, but from his observations he drew another incomplete conclusion about the nature of man. Mayo concluded that one of the greatest faults of the Industrial Revolution was that it alienated the worker from most of the experiences he held to be significant in life. The worker, Mayo believed, was demonstrating his need for belonging by his concern for acceptance in the work group over and above his economic needs. Inasmuch as scientific management had defined industrial enterprise in completely rational terms, such concern of the workers within the framework of industry had to be considered emotional or sentimental.

It therefore seemed to Mayo and other advocates of an enlarged scientific management, which now included human relations, that the worker was motivated by needs that appeared to be irrational. Management considered as rational only the worker's needs for efficiency, economic gain and humane physical treatment.

The vast difference between the manager and the worker was supposed to be that the manager would think it childish to restrict output and thereby make less money in exchange for the reward of acceptance by one's fellow workers. For the proselyte of scientific management, the manager was defined as a rational being because he can control his emotions; the worker was considered irrational because he is easily victimized by his emotions; and, in the final analysis, the worker was *by nature* inferior to the manager.

Just as the "economic man" found a pseudoscientific explanation in Darwinism, which justified his existence, so the "emotional man" found corroboration for his reason for being in the results of the Hawthorne studies. Further sanction for the view of man as controlled by his emotion was found in the growing acceptance of the theories of man's nature as abstracted from the works of Sigmund Freud.

While Freud did not discover the "emotional man," he was instrumental in defining him. Interpreters of Freudian theory said that adult behavior, particularly in its irrationalities, might be understood as manifestations of unresolved childhood needs. (What a nice fitting-in of the pieces of a jigsaw puzzle!) If the worker is a victim of his emotions and if these emotions stem from childhood, it must follow that the worker is childish. The approach of the industrial engineers comes into neat juxtaposition with the interpretations of the new psychiatry.

Chris Argyris, professor of industrial relations at Yale University, has characterized the level of work required of the worker as a result of the belief in the "mechanistic man." Argyris suggests that the child is passive, dependent and subordinate and that he is characterized further by having a short span of interest and a restricted time perspective for the meaning of his actions and by being limited in his awareness of himself as an individual.

This description fits the industrial engineer's job designs. The tasks assigned the workers were limited and sterile because it was believed that the workers were incapable of adult behavior. It seems that the worker was made to operate in an adult's body on a job that required the mentality and motivation of a child.

Argyris demonstrated this by bringing in mental patients to do an extremely routine job in a factory setting. He was rewarded by the patients' increasing the production by 400 per cent. Argyris claimed also that these mental patients worked without complaint and were most easily supervised. (This information was conveyed to the author in a personal communication.)

Scientists call this type of condition a self-confirming hypothesis. The worker is made to act like a child, and when he conforms, he is labeled a child. This is the same technique that some people use to demonstrate what they consider to be the natural inferiority of the Negro. In fact, they deny the Negro educational, social and psychological opportunities and equality with white citizens. The Negro is put into segregated schools, which are inadequately staffed and have poor physical facilities. Then, after these opportunities have been denied the Negro, the white man examines the record. The Negro does badly. This, says the white man, is proof that the Negro is inferior.

Another source of the verification of the premise that the worker is immature was the Armed Forces' psychological testing during World War I. Psychologists found that, on the average, improvement of performance in so-called intelligence tests leveled off at around the age of thirteen. On this basis, the conclusion was drawn that the average mental age of Americans was no greater than that of a thirteen-year-old child. A further deduction stemmed from other findings of the military testing program. The scores that the recruits made on the intelligence tests were shown to correlate with the level of jobs that the soldiers had held as civilians.

The erroneous conclusion, resulting from these tests, was this: If the average mentality of an American is at the thirteen-year-old level, then the mentality of the rank-and-file worker must be much below that level.

These concepts fit in nicely with the burgeoning bureaucracies that developed in order to staff the huge new production facilities. That which was applied to the rank and file moved upward to include the traditional white-collar manager and even the professional. The new problem became how to manage the managers, as if they, too, had the mentality of thirteen-year-olds. Industry had a ready set of programs based on its experience with the hourly rated rank and file that could be used if altered only slightly.

How to handle the economic motive has given rise to an unimaginable array of wage, salary, bonus and benefit programs of such intricacy that an interdisciplinary team of lawyers, economists, financiers, physicians, sociologists, psychologists and welfarists are involved in their creation, planning and administration. Research on this aspect of man is mainly at the level of new models of economic prizes, reminiscent of the frantic efforts of the giveaway shows to tantalize the audience with exotic variations of payoffs.

But the social needs of man have given rise to some of our most ingenious and, in some cases, fruitful research in industry. The problems of leadership, supervision, organizational structure, group functioning and other social-psychological issues have multiplied both our scientific and our applied literature beyond almost anything that could have been imagined a few years ago. Unfortunately, the value of this work has been detracted from by some of the evangelical zeal of its premise that man is essentially a social animal primarily in search of social gratification. The form of social criticism for this era has already been defined in the writings of David Riesman and his attack on the "lonely crowd" and in William H. Whyte's attack on the "organization man." Nevertheless, there is gold to be mined in this research for improving personnel relations, organizational efficiency and human happiness.

Closely allied with the work being done on the social psychology of industry has been the emphasis on understanding the role played by personal adjustment in the effectiveness of our industrial concerns. The clinical insights of psychiatry and psychology have become germane to the problems of people at work. The application of clinical psychiatry and psychology to industry has found expression ranging from the crude and often obnoxious misuse of personality assessment for hiring and promoting, through some of the naive psychology programs in supervisory training, to the more sophisticated managerial programs (such as the one at the Menninger Foundation) and the current wave of what may be considered a form of group therapy in sensitivity programs. Personal counseling, initiated as a product of the original Hawthorne studies, has never resulted in a promised land of psychological amelioration in industry. It is perhaps too early to forecast the impact that these newer uses of clinical psychiatry and psychology will have, but their effectiveness will be limited by the popular view of the emotionally sick man carried over from the pathological settings where the clinicians are trained. This has often led to the embarrassing necessity of labeling effective behaviors by negative terms: the well-adjusted man who earns a million dollars is overcompensating; the star football guard is a masochist sublimating an Oedipus complex.

To come to the aid of the "mechanistic man" at the managerial level, the principles of the industrial engineer were recalled and invoked. The prescriptions that followed and were offered for the ills of the managerial group were rules, regulations, policies, organizational structure, with its span and control, unity of direction, committees, "group think," etc. All of them limited human variability to ensure that no one in the managerial ranks would make a mistake.

Let me add a new definition of human nature: The "neo-mechanistic man," or, perhaps more descriptive, the "instrumental man." As the technological development of industry has moved upward, so too has the level of human activity that serves industry become involved in higher capacities. Man's higher intellectual talents must now be organized, in the same way that his motor skills were organized for assembly-line operations. The "instrumental man" is the latest model that industry has begun to market. Perhaps we have arrived at an efficient breed, a problem solver vying with the computer and caring little for who or what is responsible for the input, and caring still less for the output—other than the fact that it was achieved successfully.

It seems that every man should be a specialist, even the over-all decision makers. The satisfaction in the achievement, however, is an emotional carry-over from the previously taught psychodynamics. This new man does his job well without the intrusions of any nonspecific task-oriented factors, and it is especially important that he encapsulate what he does well from all the rest of his abilities. Precision and rationality are cardinal virtues. Every manager and professional is to be a skilled artisan (human relations, too, is a polished trade). But the joy of achievement and creativity is an unsought pleasure. The "instrumental man" finds his greatest happiness in being an unattached expert. In rereading this description, one recalls the name of Adolf Eichmann.

The behavioral scientist, including the economist, has long since debunked the concept of the "economic man," but not completely. He exists *sotto voce* in our minds, or else the importance of economic motivation has been conveniently relegated to a lower category of human needs. The same holds true for the other encompassing need-definitions of man that have proved acceptable to industry. In order of their historical appearance they include: the "physical man," whose origin is shown in industry's concern with protecting its own integrity from social protest and so providing good working conditions and fringe benefits in order to keep men contented on the job; the "mechanistic man," who delights in being used efficiently, and again, as with the concept of the "economic man," was basically a projection of industry to see human nature in the light of its own needs for efficiency; the "social man," with a prevailing desire to be acceptable to his fellow workers, and the "emotional man," who searches for psychotherapeutic environments. Industry accepted the "social man" and the "emotional man" in order to protect its growing image in the community as acknowledging the dignity of labor.

The "instrumental man" is a projection of industry's need to cope with the rationalization process that it has undertaken by incorporating advanced systems analysis and control in its operations.

Perhaps the greatest contribution that the behavioral scientists have made during the last half-century of research on the industrial scene has been to broaden the concept of the needs and nature of man from a solely economic organism to one that encompasses some of the more human aspects—the emotional and social needs.

The myths that industry has supported are not entirely invalid, but they do not tell the whole story. In fact, they tell only half the story about man's nature. These myths are stamped with the concept that man's nature is cast wholly from Adam's genes. It is wise to go back and ask once more, What is the nature of man? Not the nature of man as imposed by any particular economic or social institution, but the nature of man as it is in reality, regardless of the needs of the controlling forces.

4

The Basic Needs of Man

OF ALL THE FIELDS in which scientific thought operates, the area of human nature is the most resistant to coming to grips with reality. Mankind has been unable to maintain fictitious views of the physical universe because science has proven so many fictions to be false. The biological myths of the human body have also undergone close and careful scientific scrutiny and have succumbed proportionately to scientific understanding. But the psychological nature of man has proven difficult to catalogue, despite a longer history of speculation and despite the advantages of its having emerged as a scientific discipline after the methods of science had become clearly formulated.

A major obstacle to the formulation of natural laws regarding human behavior has been, paradoxically, the endorsement by psychologists of the efficiency of the scientific method as a means for exploration. The historical roots of psychology, the science of behavior, come from two allied disciplines—philosophy and physiology.

When scientific psychology began to develop in the late nineteenth century, it was recognized that physiology was operating on the principles of scientific method, while the other parent, philosophy, had only armchair speculation as its method of exploration. It was at this point that the psychologists insisted on a virgin birth for their field, denying their heritage from philosophy because of the latter's discredited approach to answering questions. The psychologists then proceeded to erect a psychology based essentially on the physiology and related psychology of animal behavior. In the process, the human questions that the philosophers were asking were thrown out. Man was seen to equal—not transcend—the sum of his parts.

Since then, we have learned a great deal about the psychology of Adam and have supposed that part of man's nature, inherited from Abraham, would also emerge one day as a special form of animal behavior.

The question is posed, "What is the difference between a man and an animal?" To start with, we know that man is a biological organism, and in particular is classified as an animal. Our body structure is so analogous to that of other species that it is possible to learn about functions of the human body from the study of comparative anatomy and physiology. Also, it is possible to note the changes at the different phylogenetic levels, as various species are observed, and to comprehend human development better.

Man not only bears a close relationship to animals of a simpler anatomical structure but is motivated, determined, activated and affected by the same laws of biology—the most inexorable of which is the law of evolution.

The process of evolution determines the genetic structure and physiology of the organism, and these in turn determine the behavior of the organism. (We cannot shake hands as we do by way of greeting unless we have hands that are structured to make shaking possible.) The structures that determine behavior are brought about because they prove efficacious to the survival of the organism by attuning it to the environment.

This theory had existed before the publication of Charles Darwin's *Origin of Species* in 1859. Darwin's addition to the theory was the description of the mechanism of natural selection. Evolution, Darwin concluded, leads to the design and the consequent behavior of the organism in order that it might avoid destruction.

Organisms that are constructed in a way that allows only a single, invariable, preprogrammed behavior response are thereby restricted in their survival capacity to an isometrically attuned environment. Thus an ant, a mostly precoded, determined organism, is born to do only what it is possible for an ant to accomplish. If the ant can make only one response to a situation because that is the only response built into the ant's framework, then the ant can survive only in the most rigid and restricted situation.

It is apparent that changes in the environment upset the normal life span of preprogrammed organisms, and only those survive that have either new and propitious precoded responses from biological mutations or the ability to cope with crises for which there are no instinctual responses available. Higher forms of life emerge as a result of the evolutionary process of natural selection, and at the zenith of development of adaptability stands the human being.

The evolutionary process of the human brain has prepared the organism for most activities that are not precoded. The nervous system, rather than have the behavior of each neuron stamped on it as an IBM machine perforates cards, has an opportunity to shape its function to fit a needed response.

If there is a change in the environment and if there is a pre-determined response that will be self-destructive, the brain can bring another uncoded mechanism into play to meet the threat to the organism. Typical examples of this are the dangers inherent in reacting to information obtained from our primitive sense organs, those that lead to the perception of illusions. The human brain, through education and experience, alters the response of man's behavior as a safeguard against an automatic primitive response. The human brain has the capacity to adjust to the many threats to its survival because of the myriad unassigned neurons available in the nervous system. Thus, the human animal can adapt to many situations where lower-level animals cannot.

As an illustration, there are the classic studies of conditioning originated by Ivan Pavlov. A dog's leg receives an electric shock, which causes an automatic withdrawal reflex on the part of the dog, as a response to pain. The pain the dog feels is a built-in, programmed cue that warns the dog of the possibility of destruction. The next step in the experiment adds a ringing bell at the moment of shock, so that the dog soon learns to flex at the sound of the bell. The explanation is that the dog's nervous system provides him with an unassigned nerve cell, which receives the new information. This is an indication of the dog's adaptability to change in the environment that cannot be anticipated by instinctual precoding. But the story of Pavlov's dogs has a sad ending. There is only a limited number of undetermined neurons in the dog's nervous system and thus a limited number of higher-order conditionings is possible, so that eventually the dog cannot adjust to additional threats to his existence and breaks down.

On the human level, it seems that the brain is considerably freer to adjust to the environment, having only a small part of its nervous system dedicated to instinctual responses. This is not entirely advantageous. The obvious disadvantage of an almost completely receptive nervous system is that the organism is incapable of surviving unassisted at birth. While this incompetency is characteristic of the human being, the ability to live and prosper from the extreme of the polar climates to that of the tropics—as well as in outer space—has distinct advantages in terms of survival.

Lower-level animals do not have such wide ranges of adaptability. For example, consider the behavior of animals in the presence of hunger. The need to avoid hunger is a built-in response. Animals instinctively know that hunger is a cue they must heed in order to continue life; and because the animal wishes to avoid destruction, it searches for food. Animals can be taught many other cues that signify possible hunger deprivation, such as bells ringing or, more commonly, the loss of their master's affection, but a point of no return, beyond which the animal cannot go, is soon reached.

One of the instinctual operating systems that humans possess is also the avoidance of hunger, but the hunger drive of the human system is more complex than that of other members of the animal world. When man feels hunger pangs, his impulse is to seek food. But the human precoded response to hunger becomes much more involved than the initial urge. For man has to earn money in order to purchase food, and that depends on his boss's good will. Later, when the employee has tenure and no longer worries about the loss of the boss's affection, his desire for food is complicated further by more sophisticated needs. He searches for a place where the food is specially prepared to his order, where the surroundings are pleasant and where he may be served by a pretty young waitress dressed in a bunny costume. If he cannot fulfill these specifications, he suffers from loss of appetite.

The implication is that almost anything can become a source of pain to the human organism, even a response that was originally a source of pleasure. His tremendous reservoir of carte-blanche nerve cells provides for an almost infinite number of new stimuli that can be conditioned to his primary precoded drives and thereby partake of their avoidance qualities. So, in examining the history of human experience and in cataloguing all the situations that can cause pain, it must be noted that the human being has an infinite capacity to make himself miserable.

Previously it was noted that the condition of the human brain makes it impossible for man to survive at birth without the protection and care of others. This means that the satisfaction of all the primary drives depends on the good will of parents or their surrogates.

When the human infant is hungry, the pain he suffers cannot be alleviated unless someone feeds him. If the baby is wet, he depends on someone to assuage his discomfort. If he feels in danger of falling, it is because no one is around to hold him up. Thus the baby learns to relate pain to the feeling that he is smaller and less capable than others. The human being's total inability to care for himself at birth makes a long nurturing period essential. The necessarily lengthy period of dependency continually reinforces the child's concept of his own ineffectuality, and this leads to the strengthening of the conditioned response that pain and threats to security are related to the "less than" self-concept.

We see this feeling of inferiority clearly in the teen-ager. At that time, when all the primary drives emerge in full force, he is still inhibited in their expression because the adult world suggests that he is not yet ready for his own determination. As we increase the span of the educational period, we further increase the number of reinforcements that being "less than" is a painful state. As a professor, I have learned that there is no group more inhibited than that of the twenty-five-year-old "teen-age" graduate student.

After learning that he is a dependent being, the child does not have to be consciously aware of the primary drive that instigated his feelings of malaise. The learned drives have becom functionally autonomous from the instigating primary drives. That is, the motion of a learned drive continues to exist without the force of the initial drive. It is comparable to the hunger for a particular kind of food when the body is not actually under biological duress.

Thus the condition that attaches fearful feelings of inadequacy to so many stimuli causes a great deal of pain to the individual. Man's ability to compare his situation with that of another, and to score himself as "less than" his fellow worker because he makes less money, has a smaller car and has less status, causes him to suffer greatly. Thus it is apparent that the human capacity to be unhappy is inexhaustible, because the range of stimuli that can cause pain to mankind is so vast and the number of situations in which man can make comparisons is equally inexhaustible.

It is the development of the integrative capacity of the brain by the organization of the neurons that enables human beings to cope with the tremendous input that continuing existence demands. The brain is able to integrate past, present and even future stimuli. In this sense, it has a time-binding quality that is unique in animal taxonomy.

An example from the world of work is the common event in which an employee is reprimanded by his boss. In this instance, the subordinate experiences feelings of unpleasantness, but simultaneously he recalls unpleasant situations with past authoritarian figures and anticipates possible future consequences of his employer's present anger.

As another illustration, consider an operation on the brain—the prefrontal lobotomy. When a patient was afflicted with terminal cancer and opiates could no longer control the pain, this ultimate measure used to be employed. A hole is made in the skull and the surgeon cuts the fibers running from the prefrontal cortex of the brain to the thalamic region. If, after the operation, the patient is asked, "Does it hurt?," he will answer that he has pain. But postoperative observation of the patient will show that he no longer seems to be in great stress. What the operation has accomplished is not the surcease of pain but the alleviation of suffering. The patient does not suffer, because suffering is the remembrance of past pain, the experience of present pain and the anticipation of future pain. The surgery destroys the capacity to integrate, in a time-binding fashion, the experiences of the patient. So the patient feels pain, as he does any stimulus, but he no longer suffers because he does not give a time sequence to the pain, as the brain can no longer respond to the neurons that carry that information.

Most human beings are not lobotomized—even figuratively speaking. The human being is conscious of his own consciousness, and so he remembers past pain, he experiences present pain and he anticipates future pain. Mankind is doomed to find the human condition painful and punishing because of the development of his brain. He is an organism seeking not only the surcease of pain; he is also seeking surcease from suffering.

Again, the Adam view of man appears. Not only does man suffer for his sin when he commits it, but he will also suffer in the future for the same sin, since the satisfaction of all primary drives is temporary because of their cyclical nature. Thus, if I am hungry, I will eat to alleviate my hunger and not be hungry; but I will become hungry again. If I breathe, I will have to breathe again, and so with all the body's vital functions, which we call primary drives. The needs of a higher order, such as the need for status, that are conditioned to these primary drives are characterized by the same temporary quality in the process of conditioning. The escape from pain is only temporary, whether the pain originates from a basic drive or from a more sophisticated learned drive. The human condition is a state of suffering.

How does a human differ from an animal? Quantitatively, he has a greater source of pain—he hurts more frequently; and, qualitatively, his hurt is more pressing because he experiences suffering beyond his pain.

This is the Adam view of man, in which he is bound, warped and unable to unchain the shackles of his animal nature. But it is apparent that man can in fact break the spell of a completely determined evolutionary movement. He is, in part, master of his own destiny. Man is not entirely predetermined or limited in his choices by biological laws; he is a determiner himself.

The presence of so many myopic people in the world is evidence of the ability of man himself to determine survival rather than allow the determination to be made solely by the inherited structure of the organism (via the blind and indifferent natural selection). In a situation where there has been a concerted effort to enclose all open spaces, the people with defective vision would most certainly kill themselves by running into obstructions in their paths. The law of evolution would work to eliminate these weak members of the race, and they would disappear.

But, with the invention of glasses, the near-sighted can avoid the barriers and survive to breed more myopics. Thus man's interference with evolution has made the problem of myopia inconsequential. At present, defective vision is only a problem of appearance, and contact lenses will do away with that problem as well.

It is the same with an ever-increasing number of once fatal biological mistakes. Man has broken away from the inevitability of the evolutionary principle. We are, in great part, functioning as partners with evolution; we too can participate in determining our own fates. If this is true, then man has cast his lot with the principles of cultural evolution, which has become the major determinant for human behavior.

This is in contrast to the lower animals, which are governed by predetermined laws of behavior in order to survive. The human being can survive by using his own mental abilities. Man has behavioral circuits that operate beyond the mechanisms he needs for survival. It is this surplus potentiality that engenders a separate and unique force in the motivation of the human. It is the source of the Abraham characteristic; to use one's brains is a need system of itself, divorced from any connection with, or dependence on, the basic biological stresses.

Boredom, a common human irritation, can be used as an illustration of this point. When someone is bored, there is a sensation of unpleasantness. What is the stimulus for boredom? Repetition and consistency—which constitute essentially the lack or deprivation of a stimulus. If there are feelings of listlessness and unhappiness, there must be something causing these sensations, and, though it seems paradoxical, in this case it appears to be the absence of stimuli.

The brain is an electrochemical mechanism; it has a charger and electrical impulses to keep it going, just as muscles have a certain constant potential for tonus. Similarly, the brain is constantly firing as it receives stimulation from its charger, the reticular activating system.

Man, therefore, receives internal stimulation. The nerve cells in the brain that are surplus to survival, as well as those concerned with vital functions, are being stimulated to be used, even if movement is restricted. The brain is in a state of tension, ready to work, and at the same time it is forbidden to function. This is the experience of boredom. "Stir crazy" is the prisoner's expression for his inability to express human attributes.

Nathaniel Kleitman, in *Sleep and Wakefulness* (1963), proposes in his evolutionary theory of sleep that as progression is made along the phylogenetic or ontogenetic scale, there is a greater and greater need for arousal or cortical activity: "The functional element which changes the innate primitive sleep and wakefulness alternation into the acquired advanced 24-hour sleep wakefulness is consciousness or critical reactivity."

This evolution in man begins gradually in about the third week of life, paralleling the development of thought processes and, according to Kleitman, is an inevitable consequence of the development of the ability to think. The implication is that man requires cortical stimulation (thinking) in order to stay awake beyond the time necessary to serve more than just his animalistic needs. If man is to survive as more than an animal, he must manifest and satisfy a need for cortical stimulation. Kleitman's theory is well founded empirically, and thus we have one line of empirical and theoretical evidence that indicates a biological basis for man's need to use his brains.

Another source of evidence of the need for cortical stimulation is research on sensory deprivation that refers to the elimination, reduction or stereotyping of sensory input and, because of the operation of the reticular activating system, results in decreased cortical activation. J. C. Lilly, in 1956, summarized the research findings of D. O. Hebb (who initiated much of the work on sensory deprivation) as well as his own. In Hebb's research the subject was placed on a bed in an air-conditioned box, with his arms and hands restrained by cardboard sleeves and his eyes covered with translucent ski goggles. In Lilly's studies the subject was suspended, with his body and all but the top of his head immersed in a tank containing water at 94.5° F. The subject wore a mask that covered the whole head, allowing for breathing and nothing else. The water temperature was such that the subject felt neither hot nor cold. A large fraction of the usual pressures on the body caused by gravity were lacking.

Subjects in both studies varied considerably in the details of their experiences. However, a few general phenomena appeared. After some time in the box or in the water tank, each subject found it difficult to carry on organized, directed thinking for any sustained period. Suggestibility was very much increased. An extreme desire for stimuli and action, which Lilly called a "stimulus action hunger," appeared. There were periods in which hidden methods of self-stimulation developed: twitching muscles, slow swimming movements, stroking one finger with another, etc., and, somewhat later, a more violent thrashing around to satisfy this stimulation need. The borderline between sleep and wakefulness became diffuse and confused, and if the subject remained in the situation long enough, hallucinations and delusions of various sorts occurred.

In considering the difference between an animal and a man, one should note another inexorable biological law that is pertinent to the argument—growth. By biological growth is meant the unfolding of the basic genetic substance until the organism is capable of maintaining itself. As an animal grows to biological maturity, new substrates unfold and enable new behaviors to emerge.

The animal will be able to walk, to bark and to demonstrate other behavioral patterns as soon as the biology is prepared for the specific behavior. But when biological maturity is reached, this is the approximate end of the animal's ability to increase its repertory of behavior.

As a human being grows from infancy, he also increases his biological mechanisms and learns new behaviors. A baby soon learns to walk and talk and do the multitude of things of which a child is capable when his biology is ready. But there is no sense in having a child try to ride a bicycle until certain nerve fibers become myelinated. Once this myelination is completed, the child can learn to ride a bicycle. When the human reaches biological maturity, he shares with the lower animals a tragic principle of biology, for all members of the animal kingdom wither away once the full bloom of biological maturity is reached. Thus, man begins to die at the peak of his biological development.

At this point, man again separates himself from the rest of the animal kingdom. Even as the human body senesces, man is able to grow and increase his psychological abilities. After the age of eighteen or twenty, when the body is biologically complete, man still can add psychological dimensions. This ability continues until the day he dies, as long as his body is reasonably fit. The basic distinction is that the actions of the lower animals are determined by their biological substrates, while the human animal can continue to become psychologically more active even when his biological structure is dying.

The study of the famous primate psychologists W. N. and L. A. Kellogg, in bringing up the chimpanzee Gua along with their own child, was an actual demonstration of this divergence of the abilities of man as compared with those of animals. This investigation was prompted by the controversy popular during the twenties and thirties over which was more important, genes or society, environment or heredity. The specific question was this: What would be the result of providing an ape with human nurture? The Kelloggs tried to determine the answer. They loved and handled the chimpanzee in exactly the same way as their control subject, their own son. Initially, Gua's development accelerated and preceded that of the child, primarily because the chimpanzee has a shorter life span. The child subsequently caught up with and then surpassed Gua in most behaviors; but, unlike Gua, he continued to increase his ability to enlarge his behavior repertory, to grow psychologically after maturity. While the son senesced after maturity, as his biological age advanced, he continued to grow psychologically—and, with fiction added for emphasis, might have composed *Falstaff* at the age of eighty, as Giuseppi Verdi did. If Gua had lived for eighty years (it is reported that he died of a broken heart when left by the Kelloggs), he would have achieved about the same development as he did at the age of his maturity. By then, the ape had unfolded the complete potential laid down in the DNA template of his species, this potential having nearly been reached when biological maturity was attained.

Because of man's initial animal nature, he is most sensitive to the stunting of biological growth. When a human who is physically underdeveloped is observed, his state is clearly recognized as a pathology. But when it comes to the observation of psychological immaturity, people are not so sensitive, for they are unaware that a pathology is likewise present. The potentiality of human beings is utilized at a level that is a fraction of a per cent of their capabilities; compared to cases of physical stunting, most people are psychologically unable to walk. What we have done in psychology by making comparisons between physical and mental well-being is to adopt an invalid measure for determining what is healthy.

For example, when the Chinese bound their women's feet, this was accepted as "normal" because it was the cultural norm. Yet any physician will tell you that it is pathological to walk with the foot misshapen. If it is said to be normal for people to walk around fulfilling only one iota of their human potential, then it can also be said that this is normal because it is a cultural norm. Psychologists would have to admit that this kind of reasoning is nonsensical. It is still pathological behavior, even if the culture finds it most comfortable to define it as normal.

The significance of psychological growth in the need system of human beings has two additional roots, besides the biological potential. The first root derives from the principle that biological maturity presages the onset of biological dying, and in similar fashion the cessation of psychological growth ushers in psychological dying. It is one thing to experience one's bodily decay early in life, but to be simultaneously aware that a lifetime of gradual psychological senescence lies ahead is infinitely more punishing. In order to postpone psychological oblivion, the growth period must be extended.

The second root stems from man's capacity for self-awareness, for when man is aware of himself, certain questions arise that do not arise with animals. One problem of which he is constantly aware is that of his own mortality. Man realizes that he is going to die. Also, man is aware of himself as an individual; he recognizes the truism that he is essentially alone in this world, and being alone is a rather frightening thing. He is anomic; he is separate and distinct. He is alone in a world that is indifferent to his fate. Because of this awareness, because of the ability to recognize the essential loneliness of the human condition, mankind seeks solace in metaphysical mysteries. Man needs mystery as much as he needs to know.

The primitive man who believed the winds were goblins was

physically terrified, but he was comforted by the belief that there were good goblins as well.

The history of civilization is, in part, a history of man's attempt to provide himself with comforting mysteries. But that very genius that created the mysteries by which man lives also has the power to destroy them. Every mystery that man has developed to give meaning to life has been fair game for rational analysis by man's brain. There is only one illusion that has resisted destruction. That is man's potentiality—where he can go, what he can become. This article of psychological faith gives purpose to man's existence.

To be sure, the concept of self-actualization, or self-realization, as a man's ultimate goal has been focal to the thought of many personality theorists. For such men as Jung, Adler, Sullivan, Rogers, Goldstein, Maslow and Gardner, the supreme goal of man is to fulfill himself as a creative, unique individual according to his own innate potentialities and within the limits of reality. When he is deflected from this goal, he becomes, as Jung says, "a crippled animal!"

Such a philosophy in itself, however, fails to define self-actualization or psychological growth and fails to specify the factors relevant and necessary for research progress. In the next section we shall attempt to describe the relevant criteria for psychological growth.

To summarize, the human animal has two categories of needs. One set stems from his animal disposition, that side of him previously referred to as the Adam view of man; it is centered on the avoidance of loss of life, hunger, pain, sexual deprivation, and on other primary drives, in addition to the infinite varieties of learned fears that become attached to these basic drives. The other segment of man's nature, according to the Abraham concept of the human being, is man's compelling urge to realize his own potentiality by continuous psychological growth. Perhaps there are primitive glimmerings of the Abraham characteristic in sub-human species. Recent experiments on the exploratory, curiosity and manipulative drives of animals suggest such possibilities.

If man is to be understood properly, these two characteristics must be constantly viewed as having separate biological, psychological and existential origins.

5

Psychological Growth

THE CONCEPT OF PSYCHOLOGICAL GROWTH has become increasingly important in the formulation of much psychological theory today. One of the reasons is that more attention is being given to the behavior of "normal" people pursuing their activities, a departure from the classic concern with the psychologically wounded. This means that the significance of growth in the performance of adult work has been recognized as equal in importance to, and perhaps more important than, the concern about growth in emotional development among the mentally disturbed.

Gross mental and emotional disturbance is generally screened from the business work place, and concepts that fit the clinic situation find less applicability and validity when translated to the work setting. What is needed is an understanding of normal personal growth in work equal to the understanding we find so helpful in dealing with the problems of persons with emotional retardations. The purpose of this chapter is to introduce those characteristics of psychological growth that are important for growth in job capability and performance. Those characteristics of growth are but one of many classification schemes, but they seem to relate better to understanding and assessing persons at work than do other systems.

To begin with, one of the most crucial questions to be evaluated with regard to persons is their potentiality for assuming duties of a higher order. This is by way of asking, Can they become psychologically taller than they are now? Can they grow? If a man is bright, does he act bright or merely test well? It is still necessary to know how to measure the extent to which the man is using his potential. Does he not only act bright and test well but also *indicate* that he will continue to act brighter in relation to his capacity? It is this, the process of continuation, that is important, for the essence of growth is to become more than one was before. In everyday language, does he show promise?

There are two levels of operation here. A high IQ is indicative of potential, but what is sought is an indication that the subject will use his potential. Does he show an ability for activating his possibilities? John is bright, and this suggests that he can learn to accomplish Y complexity of tasks. If he does, then of course he has fulfilled his promise. But how can this prediction be made? It is here that psychological testing is deficient; actual performance must be studied in order to make the prediction. The question is, what should be observed in performance? The answer is growth —not performance per se, but what performance indicates about his growing. For example, if you ask someone to add a column of figures and he succeeds, his performance is good, but what is known about his ability to grow? I want to make this point very clear: at the present time, testing cannot measure whether a person is growing and will continue to grow. Behavior in situations is the cue for the determination of growth. What is to be assessed is not success but whether the subject is changed for the better from the experience.

How is it known that someone is psychologically more advanced now than he was previously? The following points are grouped into what might roughly be called a cognitive category and a motivational category. They also appear in a hierarchal order, each characteristic representing a higher development of growth than the preceding one.

The first characteristic in this system is *knowing more.* Psychological testing shows that the aspect of "intelligence" least susceptible to the aging process is what man knows. While an aging man cannot run faster, and perhaps cannot add figures faster or remember longer series of digits, he can add more information and knowledge to that which he already possesses. It is true that more is forgotten, but the point is that man can learn more.

The first level of psychological growth establishes whether there is a difference today from yesterday in what one knows. The man who says "I haven't learned anything in ten years" is saying that a ruler put to his accumulation of knowledge would measure the same as before. The fact is that he is only dying psychologically—forgetting, and thereby psychologically diminishing. This applies equally to the person whose only change in what he knows is the name of the current Western television program and to the college professor who lectures from the proverbial frayed notes assembled years ago.

Every job experience consists, in part, of the familiar plus some of the unfamiliar; this means that some tasks can be done without a person's knowing anything more than was known before, while other tasks require some learning of new facts and principles. Even if these new facts are not essential or even directly related to the task at hand, they may nevertheless be useful for later tasks. It is in the exposure to the unfamiliar that we look for evidence of psychological growth. Is it not legitimate to ask, after a job assignment, whether an employee has learned anything— has he in this case added to what he knows? For success does not necessarily accompany psychological growth, while very often failure gives rise to considerable growth. To be sure, all tasks do not provide much in the way of the unfamiliar, particularly because jobs today are so very much overstructured.

It is equally important to stress the overdeterminism that can be seen in the world of work. Often, it can be a rationalization, a means of avoiding the effort of psychological growth, to add blinders to the already heavily structured job tasks. All situations can lead to an increase in what can be known. Individuals surely differ in what they absorb from an experience—first, with respect to quantity and, second, along a dimension of quality, relevancy or importance.

It is these differences among individuals that permit assessment. There are individuals who walk out knowing only what they knew before, and those who have picked up only such new knowledge as was necessary to performance in the job. However, those workers who have picked up surplus knowledge also vary in what they have shown for the capacity to grow psychologically. It is obvious that the assessment of growth depends on how well the supervisor or the evaluator knows what the job involves and is himself perceptive enough to recognize that his subordinate has learned something of which he was previously unaware. It is also true that the mealy assignment leads to little growth and forces evaluations on the basis of factors irrelevant to much future success—such as evaluating peripheral personality characteristics.

The second characteristic of psychological growth to be considered is more *relationships in knowledge*. Symbolically, this characteristic may be stated as follows: I can know A and I can know B, but do I ever see that they may be related? In other words, how much of what I learn is kept in discrete isolated bits, and to what extent do I relate what I learn to past learning or to another contemporary addition to my information? In philosophical terms, this characteristic may be called the development of wisdom. "Idiot savant," or "wise idiot," is a term in psychology describing an individual who has an ability to regurgitate a specific amount of information without comprehension of its meaning. Some individuals—a television quiz program contestant, for example—can similarly regurgitate a wealth of discrete information in many areas, again, however, without much comprehension or systematization of his knowledge. It is possible to acquire isolated bits of information, but a growing individual tries to place new information in context by relating it to other information. In practice, the distinction shows itself when one person, in describing a job experience, can give a "picture" of the situation while another sees only the trees. These two individuals might be equal in terms of the first characteristic of psychological growth, i.e., adding knowledge, but they part ways on this higher level of cognitive development.

In science, facts are uncovered; these facts are then related to principles, principles to laws and laws to theories—all in an attempt to deal with more phenomena in the most economic fashion and with the greatest effectiveness. Inasmuch as each fact or principle operates in conjunction with other facts and principles, failure to see interrelationships will lead to ineffective practice, despite high competence in understanding and using any one fact.

The third characteristic of psychological growth is *creativity*. The human brain is capable of taking in an infinite amount of bits of information and can connect these bits in order to store principles of relationships as well. However, the brain is not only an input system—its most remarkable characteristic is its ability to emit new knowledge and principles. It takes in bits of information and makes relationships and further uses these as grist for its own manufacturing or creative processes. Animals are almost solely determined by imprinted systems and are therefore limited by brain connections already laid down, but the human brain, in addition, makes its own world, to which it reacts. All cultural artifacts are products of man's creativity, inasmuch as they do not exist in nature without man's intervention.

For a human it would be impossible to survive if there were dependence only on that information that was specifically taught, for the range of situations that occur and the knowledge that is required in the simplest of daily activities call for an immense addition to the store of information. Creativity is therefore a concept not limited to the spectacular or original, in the sense of what is new to mankind, but rather it encompasses any knowledge, understanding or principle that originates with the individual. This new knowledge may be of the "garden variety," as most of it is, since all people live with common stimuli for their inputs of knowledge. The term "insight" is sometimes used to express "nonoriginal" creativity by the individual, suggesting that the concept is common knowledge; but the individual now has achieved recognition of this new fact or principle, which is new to him, and so he has grown.

If growth is defined in terms of the utilization of potentiality, then the individual who minimizes the potential of the brain by failing to use its manufacturing properties is one who is not growing at this level. "The only thing I know is what I read in the newspaper." "No one ever told me." These statements suggest an individual who is passive at the cognitive level, passive in the sense that he is dependent on other brains for what he has to do; his own brain needs to be plugged into an outside feeding circuit, since it is a dependent, rather than an active and independent, brain.

Each experience includes some novel or unfamiliar characteristic. It is from the unfamiliar that the fund of information and relationships can be most increased, giving man the opportunity to utilize his creative potentiality. Creativity can be achieved even within familiar settings, despite the fact that in such situations the brain can relax and coast on previously learned reactions. How comfortable it is to be able to earn a living today on yesterday's knowledge, but how often this leads to obsolescence. Moreover, challenging assignments are as much defined by what the worker puts into them as by what has been put in for him. An evaluation of the creativity of a subordinate requires assignments that do not have built-in solutions or responses. At the same time, there must be an awareness that what is built-in is very often as much the perception of an uncreative mind as of the actual situation. Some people are determined; some are determiners. The determiners use their brains for dynamic, creative activity, while the determined are unable to do so.

The next set of characteristics relate more to the psychological growth of the individual in terms of his motivation. Does he wish to be mature and derive satisfaction from becoming an adult? The fourth characteristic of psychological growth is *effectiveness in ambiguity*. The world is ambiguous and perhaps probabilistic; uncertainty pervades our living experience. Part of the penalty we pay for our emergence from the lower-animal status is our awareness of the lack of certitude in our lives. In some ways this is a penalty and a source of much anxiety, but from the Abraham view it is the reward for being human because it adds challenge, variety and opportunity to existence.

Children, however, cannot cope with all the ambiguity that adults must handle. The child's immaturity in dealing with the uncertainty of the world causes the parents and their representatives to protect him. This protection serves to dispel the ambiguity and reassure the need for absolutes, unconditionals, perfections and predictabilities. The child's biological survival depends on absolutes; his psychological comfort requires predictabilities. When the child is no longer under the wing of his parents, does he learn to blunder alone through the maze of incongruities, or does he seek parental substitutes? The paradox is that just as the child becomes aware of the world's ambiguity, that is the moment when he must make his own decisions. Parents make decisions for their offspring, and they make them in a such a way as to indicate to their children that order and absolutes are the natural framework of life. Children are excused for mistakes in decision making, but as adults their actions are expected to be effective. Therefore, emergence from childhood entails toleration and effectiveness in ambiguity.

This is one of the most difficult challenges in growing up—to live with insecurity, to accept change and alteration, to deal with complexity. Inasmuch as complexity and change constitute a more real phenomenon than do absolutes and finalities, it becomes necessary to seek further complications in order to get closer to reality and away from the fiction of a child's world.

To put this characteristic of effectiveness in ambiguity symbolically, a child can make a decision between A and B, a two-variable problem, by encapsulating the problem from the complexity of C, D, E, etc., which are the other variables that would serve to complicate his decision making. This process of encapsulating the problem does violence to reality, and because of this the child's decisions are restricted to those of little consequence. However, adults deal with decisions of greater moment and cannot afford the luxury of a restriction in the field that defines our problems. At the same time, adults are *required* to make decisions, for as mature individuals they must stand on their own merits. Everyone is familiar with those people who perpetuate their childish demand for simplicity of action by surrendering their adult status to an authority figure who can make decisions. This process provides security to those who hold a childish view of the world. These persons are fair game for the demagogue, who represents the strength and protection that daddy gave them.

However, another approach to maintaining the security of the childish world is to internalize what daddy appeared to represent. That is, to continue to look at the world in the same way that daddy represented it to be. This can be done in two ways. First, the nervous system can be blocked off in order to shut out anything that provides for dissonance or complexity. "Don't tell me any more; it is complex enough!" By his own volition, man succeeds in seeing the world as he saw it in his childhood. Our eyes get bigger, but we learn to squint—to avoid troublesome data.

A parallel technique is to overgeneralize. "I see no difference between A and B and C and D." Therefore, a four-variable problem is reduced to a two-variable problem, and decisions are easier because the complexity has been reduced. What happens to the effectiveness of such people? An example from my experience as a teacher may serve to illustrate this point.

I am required to give examinations at the close of the academic year. Because of my own laziness, and perhaps because I wish to be more objective in grading, I give a multiple-choice test, in which each item consists of a stem and four possible answers: A, B, C and D. Now, a student taking this examination reads the stem and then reads choice A. He says to himself, "I see what he is asking and this answer makes sense." Then he looks at choice B and realizes that the question was a bit more complex than he had thought at first, for I have brought in additional variables to be considered. After thinking for a while, he decides that he can make a choice between A and B. Then he looks at choice C, and perhaps mutters an invective, for he now realizes that the answer to the question is becoming more complex, since I have introduced a third variable for his consideration. When he finally looks at D, he throws up his hands in despair, for now rather than make a choice based on a simple variable, he has to juggle at least four variables to come to a decision. This is too much for him, but at the same time he is required to make a decision; his grade depends on his making a choice. What can he do? A solution offered earlier was to block off the nervous system against new and complicating facts. The student can accomplish this by covering up all C and D choices and choosing between only A and B answers. Ambiguity is thus reduced to a point at which he finds he can make decisions. But with what effect? It is obvious that he will receive the lowest grade in the class, because his maximum score will be 50 per cent (assuming a random dispersion of the correct answers among the four choices).

Often such people are referred to as narrow-minded, short-sighted and, in a misuse of the term, conservative. When such individuals are prominent in the social and political sphere, we may object to them on value grounds. Such objections are more rationally made on the basis that their solutions to problems will be ineffective, because these narrow-minded people are acting from a view of situations that have been simplified to meet their needs rather than the actual needs of the question at issue. The inability to tolerate ambiguity must then lead to ineffectiveness, and it is the ineffectiveness that is evaluated and provides the cue to the failure of psychological growth in this dimension.

It is a trend in modern industry to engineer all ambiguity out of jobs and render them suitable to a child's ability. Such an orientation to the structure of work can serve only to reinforce an immature dependency on the lack of ambiguity. The maturing individual recognizes the temporary nature of the answers provided in overstructured jobs. He sees that the greatest reality of all is change, and he is less likely to succumb to the temptation of looking at and handling situations in a sophomoric way. If many assignments are defined by the worker as routine, this may suggest a lack of growth. Too much overgeneralization from one situation to another suggests a lack of growth. Too much passivity, along with feelings of determinism, suggests a lack of growth. Too much impatience in problem solving, leading to action for action's sake—action to obviate the need for deeper consideration —also suggests a lack of growth.

The fifth characteristic of psychological growth is *individuation*. The principle of individuation is one of the basic rules of biological growth. Life begins as an undifferentiated mass, and through various stages of development each body system (as well as the components within that system) individuates as a separate functioning unit. Psychological growth also proceeds from an undifferentiated mass of sensation and behavior (the buzzing confusion of the infant world described by William James) to separate and distinct areas of sensation and behavior.

In the same manner, the individual begins life as a part of a social unit, the family, and remains as part of the group until he is socially and legally mature. Then he becomes further immersed in other social units. We call this process socialization, which is the practice of making sure that each of us formally blends into his own particular society. Society requires that we regiment the child and make him look and behave in ways no different from those of other children. We dress more or less alike; speak more or less alike; eat more or less alike; learn mostly the same things, and have similar manners, beliefs, customs, ideas, aspirations, morals, ethics, rituals, humor, indignations, fears, values, games and so on. We are molded into the All-American Boy, the Soviet Comrade, the English Gentleman, the Sioux Brave and the like. Man becomes a member of a family; then a student in a school; a part of social, ethnic, religious and work organizations of the neighborhood, of the region and of the country, and finally a member of the brotherhood of man—until there is no longer any area for individual response to life.

Why has the process of individuation been reversed when it comes to the total human organism? Why is the individual continually immersed in more and more groups, with the consequence of less personal identity? The answer is that, without such a process, the very biological integrity of the child would be jeopardized; he must learn to exist in an interpersonal environment made up of people and human institutions. Boys wearing dresses in school would not survive; using a dinner fork in the English manner would lead to severe social censure, and teenagers, who find the tyranny of the peer group at its maximum, strive for conformity as if their very lives depended on it. Thus the child is protected; he is taught the ropes for existing in this environment, and his predecessors' knowledge and experience are passed on, in order that he may cope with life.

The primal fact is that each human being is separate, distinct, and a unique individual, with a nervous system as particular as are fingerprints. There is no organic connection between individuals after the umbilical cord is cut; all connections become the inventions and delusions of man. Each individual is basically alone and he will die alone; the only exception is Siamese twins, and this exception exists because there is an organic connection. We say that growing up is painful, that it is hard. Why? The maximum security is in the womb, where the greatest symbiosis exists and where there is also the lowest level of human existence. If man is not separate, and thereby alone, he does not fully exist and his fears are therefore reduced proportionately. The continuation of the socialization process beyond that necessary for man's becoming fully aware of the world in which he lives represents nothing more than partial suicide. The anxiety that a separate individual must automatically face is exchanged for the comfortable companionship of the herd.

Suppose, as an example, you are asked to identify yourself. Essentially the question is: Who are you? Here are a few possible responses: "I am an engineer for X.Y. & Z." "I am a member of the Rotary." "I am the owner of a Buick." "I am a member of the Rising Waters Country Club." "I am a husband and a father." If all these identities are placed on cards against a black curtain, with a separate spotlight focused on each of them, a game of blackouts can be played. Take the first identity, that of an engineer for X.Y. & Z. He loses his job with the company; that spotlight is dimmed and that identity blacked out on the curtain. Next, the engineer's children grow up and fail to send him a postcard on Father's Day; again a light goes out. The wife of the engineer from X.Y. & Z. leaves him for the man who fired him; another light goes out. In looking for another job, he resigns from the local Rotary and the Country Club; two more lights are extinguished. Finally, the poor engineer cannot afford the Buick, and the last light goes out. Now look at the curtain. It can be seen that the engineer has disappeared, that he does not exist, that there is nothing there. But this is manifestly absurd, because obviously there is a biological hulk still occupying space. This is the tragedy. Biological space is being filled, but a psychological presence is lacking. This is the existentialist nonbeing.

One of the highest levels of psychological growth is becoming an individual—desocializing and separating the individual from his environment, as his organic condition suggests is a natural thing to do. This means a man's having, in addition to what the socialization process makes of him, his own feelings, beliefs, values, judgments, ideas and behaviors, as a mark that he himself exists and not merely as a protest to society. Cooperation with others becomes a means not only of enhancing some fictitious entity, the group, but also of personal enhancement. Cooperation as a procedure of compromise is a means of achieving a goal at the expense of mutual amputation.

Does the mature person show loyalty to the group and, in this instance, to the company? If being an X Company man means that he exists as an engineer, for example, only when a company modifier is attached to his profession, then the answer is emphatically no. Does he thrill to being included in the X Company family, regardless of what he is doing on the job? Again the answer is an emphatic no. Is loyalty based on the opportunity within X Company to become greater in knowledge, relationships, creativity and living, as well as to be effective in ambiguity and to become independent of the company for his own meaning? Here the answer is an equally emphatic yes.

How can psychological growth be evaluated in terms of this characteristic? It depends on whether a separate person or a component part of an organization is to be considered.

The sixth characteristic of psychological growth is *real growth*. Let me introduce the concept by a familar game that children play. It goes by many names, but it used to be called "playing house." There are many variations, the improvisations always making it a fresh experience for children, with all the nuances of adult behavior and events that can be mimed. Very often a child will dress in mommy's or daddy's clothes and pretend he is grown up. If, however, after the game the child's clothes are removed so he can be bathed, he will displace the same amount of water as before. His "growth" was only illusory, but at the time the child really felt taller, and this is the important psychological point. Illusion and reality are not clearly differentiated in a child, but he is protected from the consequences by the sophistication and the intervention of adults.

One of the most difficult surrenders that people are forced to make when they grow up is to cleave fantasy from the real, to stamp it as fiction to be used only for recreation. Since all things are possible in fantasy, is it any wonder that this characteristic of growth has deep and firm roots? A peculiar quirk seems to take place in the adult approach to unreality. One would think that if it is so easy to spot the illusions of children, it should be equally easy to grasp the illusions of adults.

Strangely, the reverse is true. Adults are incredibly blind. Perhaps this is because adult illusions are most pronounced in the area of self-awareness or self-concept. Men can strip themselves of the mysteries that attach to their conceptions of the physical universe, of their own bodies, even of their religious beliefs, but what they cannot give up are the illusions of who they are.

In a society as complex and fluid as ours, there is a plethora of symbols that act the way daddy's clothes do for the child; that is, they reflect back to the viewer elongated and distorted pictures of how tall he is, in the manner of the trick mirrors in carnivals. Job titles, appurtenances of rank, social courtesies, organizational structure, relationships with others, the ownership of the myriad of status gadgets—all these and more serve as substitutes for substantive accretion to psychological tissue, and thereby deceive one into believing he is taller than he really is. But these "clothes" are fitted with the strongest of epoxy glues; rather than come off at night, they adhere and thus divert necessary energies away from real growth.

Of all the means by which artificial growth takes place, perhaps the most ubiquitous and damaging is that of degrading others so that it is possible to look better in comparison, or of standing on others to gain height. Success can be had in this direction—witness the empathy and understanding that *How to Succeed in Business Without Really Trying* has achieved. Yet the piper must be paid. Executives who climb to the top on such shadows find, when they get there, that more than shadows are needed for the tasks they face, with the consequence of physical and mental distress that calls forth the plaintive question, Is success worth it? Assuredly success is worthwhile to those who achieved their positions of responsibility on the basis of real growth.

Another subtle way in which it is possible to grow at the expense of others is to bask in their reflected glory. The mother whose only self-significance lies in her son "the doctor," the professor who rests content on the success of his students, the wife who lives her life through her husband and the boss who compensates for his own substantive lack by counting his blessings in terms of those he has developed—all are playing the same charade. As a psychologist, I have as much sympathy and understanding for human weakness as the next person, but I cannot mistake human weakness for human strength. I am well aware that honors are due those who assist others in their growth, but it is a delusion to believe that you can claim part of someone else's growth as yours. Growth at the expense of others merely diminishes them; it does not add to your psychological tissue.

In summary, the six points of psychological growth are knowing more, seeing more relationships in what we know, being creative, being effective in ambiguous situations, maintaining individuality in the face of the pressures of the group and attaining real psychological growth. All of these factors can be recognized as the Abraham view of man, that is, the necessity to realize the human potential for perfection. This is contrary to the Adam view of man, which sees the human being as characterized by the need to avoid physical deprivation.

6

The Motivation-
Hygiene Theory

WITH THE DUALITY of man's nature in mind, it is well to return to the significance of these essays to industry by reviewing the motivation-hygiene concept of job attitudes as it was reported in *The Motivation to Work*. This study was designed to test the concept that man has two sets of needs: his need as an animal to avoid pain and his need as a human to grow psychologically.

For those who have not read *The Motivation to Work*, I will summarize the highlights of that study. Two hundred engineers and accountants, who represented a cross-section of Pittsburgh industry, were interviewed. They were asked about events they had experienced at work which either had resulted in a marked improvement in their job satisfaction or had led to a marked reduction in job satisfaction.

The interviewers began by asking the engineers and accountants to recall a time when they had felt exceptionally good about their jobs. Keeping in mind the time that had brought about the good feelings, the interviewers proceeded to probe for the reasons why the engineers and accountants felt as they did. The workers were asked also if the feelings of satisfaction in regard to their work had affected their performance, their personal relationships and their well-being.

Finally, the nature of the sequence of events that served to return the workers' attitudes to "normal" was elicited. Following the narration of a sequence of events, the interview was repeated, but this time the subjects were asked to describe a sequence of events that resulted in negative feelings about their jobs. As many sequences as the respondents were able to give were recorded within the criteria of an acceptable sequence. These were the criteria:

First, the sequence must revolve around an event or series of events; that is, there must be some objective happening. The report cannot be concerned entirely with the respondent's psychological reactions or feelings.

Second, the sequence of events must be bound by time; it should have a beginning that can be identified, a middle and, unless the events are still in process, some sort of identifiable ending (although the cessation of events does not have to be dramatic or abrupt).

Third, the sequence of events must have taken place during a period in which feelings about the job were either exceptionally good or exceptionally bad.

Fourth, the story must be centered on a period in the respondent's life when he held a position that fell within the limits of our sample. However, there were a few exceptions. Stories involving aspirations to professional work or transitions from subprofessional to professional levels were included.

Fifth, the story must be about a situation in which the respondent's feelings about his job were directly affected, not about a sequence of events unrelated to the job that caused high or low spirits.

Figure 1, reproduced from *The Motivation to Work*, shows the major findings of this study. The factors listed are a kind of shorthand for summarizing the "objective" events that each respondent described. The length of each box represents the frequency with which the factor appeared in the events presented. The width of the box indicates the period in which the good or bad job attitude lasted, in terms of a classification of short duration and long duration. A short duration of attitude change did not last longer than two weeks, while a long duration of attitude change may have lasted for years.

Five factors stand out as strong determiners of job satisfaction —*achievement, recognition, work itself, responsibility* and *ad-*

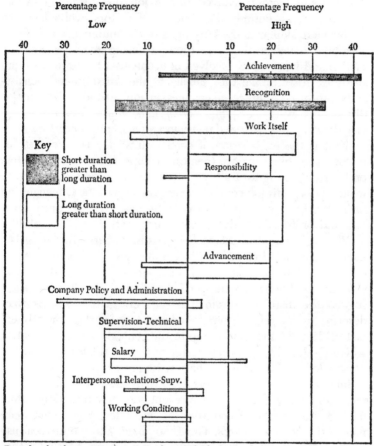

Figure 1

Comparison of Satisfiers and Dissatisfiers

Reproduced with permission from F. Herzberg *et al. The Motivation to Work.* John Wiley and Sons, New York, 1959.

vancement—the last three being of greater importance for lasting change of attitudes. These five factors appeared very infrequently when the respondents described events that paralleled job dissatisfaction feelings. A further word on *recognition:* when it appeared in a "high" sequence of events, it referred to recognition for achievement rather than to recognition as a human-relations tool divorced from any accomplishment. The latter type of recognition does not serve as a "satisfier."

When the factors involved in the job dissatisfaction events were coded, an entirely different set of factors evolved. These factors were similar to the satisfiers in their unidimensional effect. This time, however, they served only to bring about job dissatisfaction and were rarely involved in events that led to positive job attitudes. Also, unlike the "satisfiers," the "dissatisfiers" consistently produced short-term changes in job attitudes. The major dissatisfiers were *company policy and administration, supervision, salary, interpersonal relations* and *working conditions.*

What is the explanation of such results? Do the two sets of factors have two separate themes? It appears so, for the factors on the right of Figure 1 all seem to describe man's relationship to what he does: his job content, achievement on a task, recognition for task achievement, the nature of the task, responsibility for a task and professional advancement or growth in task capability.

What is the central theme for the dissatisfiers? Restating the factors as the kind of administration and supervision received in doing the job, the nature of interpersonal relationships and working conditions that surround the job and the effect of salary suggest the distinction from the "satisfier" factors. Rather than describe man's relationship to what he does, the "dissatisfier" factors describe his relationship to the context or environment in which he does his job. One cluster of factors relates to what the person does and the other to the situation in which he does it.

Since the dissatisfier factors essentially describe the environment and serve primarily to prevent job dissatisfaction, while having little effect on positive job attitudes, they have been named the *hygiene* factors. This is an analogy to the medical use of the term meaning "preventative and environmental." Another term for these factors in current use is *maintenance* factors. I am indebted to Dr. Robert Ford of the American Telephone and Telegraph Company for this excellent synonym. The "satisfier" factors were named the *motivators,* since other findings of the study suggest that they are effective in motivating the individual to superior performance and effort.

So far, I have described that part of the interview that was restricted to determining the actual objective events as reported by the respondents (first level of analysis). They were also asked to interpret the events, to tell why the particular event led to a change in their feelings about their jobs (second level of analysis). The principal result of the analysis of this data was to suggest that the hygiene or maintenance events led to job dissatisfaction because of a need to *avoid* unpleasantness; the motivator events led to job satisfaction because of a need for growth or self-actualization. At the psychological level, the two dimensions of job attitudes reflected a two-dimensional need structure: one need system for the avoidance of unpleasantness and a parallel need system for personal growth.

The discussion so far has paved the way for the explanation of the duality of job-attitude results. Why do the hygiene factors serve as dissatisfiers? They represent the environment to which man the animal is constantly trying to adjust, for the environment is the source of Adam's suffering. The hygiene factors listed are the major environmental aspects of work.

Why do the motivators affect motivation in the positive direction? An analogy drawn from a familiar example of psychological growth in children may be useful. When a child learns to ride a bicycle, he is becoming more competent, increasing the repertory of his behavior, expanding his skills—psychologically growing. In the process of the child's learning to master a bicycle, the parents can love him with all the zeal and compassion of the most devoted mother and father. They can safeguard the child from injury by providing the safest and most hygienic area in which to practice; they can offer all kinds of incentives and rewards, and they can provide the most expert instructions. But the child will never, never learn to ride the bicycle—unless he is given a bicycle! The hygiene factors are not a valid contributor to psychological growth. The substance of a task is required to achieve growth goals. Similarly, you cannot love an engineer into creativity, although by this approach you can avoid his dissatisfactions with the way you treat him. Creativity will require a potentially creative task to do.

In summary, two essential findings were derived from this study. First, the factors involved in producing job satisfaction were *separate* and *distinct* from the factors that led to job dissatisfaction. Since separate factors needed to be considered, depending on whether job satisfaction or job dissatisfaction was involved, it followed that these two feelings were not the obverse of each other. Thus, the opposite of job satisfaction would not be job dissatisfaction, but rather *no* job satisfaction; similarly, the opposite of job dissatisfaction is *no* job dissatisfaction, not satisfaction with one's job. The fact that job satisfaction is made up of two unipolar traits is not unique, but it remains a difficult concept to grasp.

Perhaps another analogy will help explain this new way of thinking about job attitudes. Let us characterize job satisfaction as vision and job dissatisfaction as hearing. It is readily seen that we are talking about two separate dimensions, since the stimulus for vision is light, and increasing and decreasing light will have no effect on man's hearing. The stimulus for audition is sound, and, in a similar fashion, increasing or decreasing loudness will have no effect on vision.

Man's basic needs can be diagrammed as two parallel arrows pointing in opposite directions. One arrow depicts his Animal-Adam nature, which is concerned with avoidance of pain stemming from the environment, and for man the psychological environment is the major source of this pain. The other arrow represents man's Human-Abraham nature, which is concerned with approaching self-fulfillment or psychological growth through the accomplishment of tasks.

Animal-Adam—Avoidance of Pain from Environment

←————————————————————————————

Human-Abraham—Seeking Growth from Tasks

————————————————————————————→

The problem of establishing a zero point in psychology, with the procedural necessity of using instead a bench mark (e.g., the mean of a population) from which to start our measurement, has led to the conception that psychological traits are bipolar. Recent empirical investigations, however, have cast some shadows on the assumptions of bipolarity for many psychological attributes, in addition to job attitudes, as shown in *The Motivation to Work*.

Thus, the hypothesis with which the study of motivation began appears to be verified. The factors on the right of Figure 1 that led to satisfaction (*achievement, recognition, work itself, responsibility* and *advancement*) are mainly unipolar; that is, they contribute very little to job dissatisfaction. Conversely, the dissatisfiers (*company policy and administration, supervision, interpersonal relations, working conditions* and *salary*) contribute very little to job satisfaction.

Sixteen separate job-attitude factors were investigated in the original study dealing with accountants and engineers. Only those motivators and hygiene factors that were found to differentiate statistically between positive and negative job attitudes were presented. However, the other factors have similarly been shown to fall into one category or the other in the follow-up studies to be described in subsequent chapters. These factors are *possibility of growth*, a task-centered motivator, and the hygiene factors, *salary, status, job security* and *effect on personal life*.

In Chapter 2, I indicated a desire to define a human being and in the following sections I have attempted to organize man's needs to reach such a definition. Since man is capable of such a variety of behavior and still can survive, it is little wonder that so many ways of acting can be declared normal, dependent on their cultural acceptance. In this sense, a prominent difference between cultures lies in the kinds of pathology that are declared normal. At this point, the theory of job motivation will be expanded to a general concept of mental health, and this in turn will allow for a culture-free definition of mental illness.

Just as there are two sets of needs at work—hygiene needs and motivator needs—and two continua to represent them, so we may speak of two continua in mental health: a mental-illness continuum and a mental-health continuum. We have seen that a conceptual shift in viewpoint regarding job attitudes has been made in order to incorporate the two-dimensional motivation-hygiene theory. Essentially the same shift might well lead to an equally important change in theory and research on mental health.

The argument for this generalization has been presented in two papers by Dr. Roy Hamlin of the Veterans Administration and myself. The implications for mental health are best introduced by recalling the subjective reactions of the employees as to why the various factors affected them as they did. For the job-dissatisfied situation the subjects reported that they were made unhappy mostly because they felt they were being treated unfairly or that they found the situation unpleasant or painful. On the other hand, the common denominator for the reasons for positive job attitudes seemed to be variations on the theme of feelings of psychological growth, the fulfillment of self-actualizing needs. There was an approach-avoidance dichotomy with respect to job adjustment. A need to avoid unpleasant job environments led to job dissatisfaction; the need for self-realization led to job satisfaction when the opportunity for self-realization was afforded.

A "hygienic" environment prevents discontent with a job, but such an environment cannot lead the individual beyond a minimal adjustment consisting of the absence of dissatisfaction. A positive "happiness" seems to require some attainment of psychological growth.

It is clear why the hygiene factors fail to provide for positive satisfactions: they do not possess the characteristics necessary for giving an individual a sense of growth. To feel that one has grown depends on achievement in tasks that have meaning to the individual, and since the hygiene factors do not relate to the task, they are powerless to give such meaning to the individual. Growth is dependent on some achievements, but achievement requires a task. The motivators are task factors and thus are necessary for growth; they provide the psychological stimulation by which the individual can be activated toward his self-realization needs.

To generalize from job attitudes to mental attitudes, we can think of two types of adjustment for mental equilibrium. First, an adjustment to the environment, which is mainly an avoidance adjustment; second, an adjustment to oneself, which is dependent on the successful striving for psychological growth, self-actualization, self-realization or, most simply, being psychologically more than one has been in the past.

Traditionally, mental health has been regarded as the obverse of mental illness. Mental health, in this sense, is the mere *absence* of mental illness. At one time, the psychiatrist anticipated that mental health would be automatically *released* when the conflicts of mental illness were resolved. And, currently, the biochemist hopes that mental health will bloom once neuroenzymes are properly balanced and optimally distributed in the brain.

In essence, this traditional view ignores *mental health*. In general, the focus has been on mental illness—on anxiety, anxiety-reducing mechanisms, past frustrations, childhood trauma, distressing interpersonal relations, disturbing ideas and worries, current patterns of inefficiency and stressful present environment. Except for sporadic lip service, positive attitudes and experiences have been considered chiefly in an atmosphere of alleviating distress and dependency.

The factors that determine mental illness are *not the obverse* of the mental health factors. Rather, the mental illness factors belong to the category of hygiene factors, which describe the environment of man and serve to cause illness when they are deficient but effect little positive increase in mental health. They are factors that cause avoidance behavior; yet, as will be explained, only in the "sick" individual is there an attempt to activate approach behavior. The implications of the conceptual shift for job satisfaction have been discussed. Traditional research on job attitudes has focused almost exclusively on only one set of factors, on the hygiene or job-context factors. The motivating factors, the positive or self-actualizing factors, have been largely neglected. The thesis holds that a very similar neglect has characterized traditional research on mental health.

Specifically, the resolution of conflicts, the correction of biochemical imbalance and the modification of psychic defenses might all be assigned to the attempts to modify the hygiene or avoidance needs of the individual. The positive motivating factors—self-actualization and personal growth—have received treatment of two sorts. Either they have been neglected or dismissed as irrelevant, or they have been regarded as so individually sacred and vague as to defy research analysis. At best, the mental health factors have been looked upon as important *forces* that might be released by the removal of mental illness factors.

The motivation-hygiene concept stresses three points regarding mental adjustment. The first is the proposition that mental illness and mental health are not of the same dimension. Contrary to classical psychiatric belief, there are degrees of sickness and there are degrees of health. The degree of sickness reflects an individual's reaction to the hygiene factors, while the degree of mental health represents his reaction to the motivator factors.

Second, the motivator-mental-health aspect of personal adjustment has been sadly neglected in theory, in research and in application. The positive side of personal adjustment has been considered to be a dividend or consequence of successful attention to the "negative-maladjustment" side.

The third point is a new definition or idea of mental illness. The new definition derives from the first proposition that mental illness is not the opposite of mental health, as is suggested by some of the data on job satisfaction.

While the incidents in which job satisfaction were reported almost always contained the factors that related to the job task—the motivators—there were some individuals who reported receiving job satisfaction solely from hygiene factors, that is, from some aspect of the job environment. Commenting on this reversal, the authors of *The Motivation to Work* suggest that "there may be individuals who because of their training and because of the things that have happened to them have learned to react positively to the factors associated with the *context* of their jobs." The hygiene seekers are primarily attracted to things that usually serve only to prevent dissatisfaction, not to be a source of positive feelings. The hygiene seekers have not reached a stage of personality development at which self-actualizing needs are active. From this point of view, they are fixated at a less mature level of personal adjustment.

Implied in *The Motivation to Work* is the admonition to industry that the lack of "motivators" in jobs will increase the sensitivity of employees to real or imagined bad job hygiene, and consequently the amount and quality of hygiene given to employees must be constantly improved. There is also the reported finding that the relief from job dissatisfaction by hygiene factors has only a temporary effect and therefore adds to the necessity for more frequent attention to the job environment. The graphs shown in Figure 1 indicate that the hygiene factors stem from short-range events, as contrasted with the longer range of motivator events. It will be recalled in Chapter 4, on the basic needs of man, that animal or hygiene drives, being cyclical, are only temporarily satisfied. The cyclical nature of these drives is necessary in order to sustain life. The hygiene factors on the job partake of the quality of briefly acting analgesics for meaningless work; the individual becomes unhappy without them, but is relieved only temporarily with them, for their effects soon wear off and the hygiene seeker is left chronically dissatisfied.

A hygiene seeker is not merely a victim of circumstances, but is *motivated* in the direction of temporary satisfaction. It is not that his job offers little opportunity for self-actualization; rather, it is that his needs lie predominantly in another direction, that of satisfying avoidance needs. He is seeking positive happiness via the route of avoidance behavior, and thus his resultant chronic dissatisfaction is an illness of motivation. Chronic unhappiness, a motivation pattern that insures continual dissatisfaction, a failure to grow or to want to grow—these characteristics add up to a neurotic personality.

So it appears that the neurotic is an individual with a lifetime pattern of hygiene seeking and that the definition of a neurotic, in terms of defenses against anxiety arising from early psychological conflicts, represents at best the *origin* of his hygiene seeking. The motivation-hygiene view of a neurotic adjustment is free of substantial ties with any theory of etiology, and therefore the thesis is independent of conceptualizations regarding the traditional dynamics of personality development and adjustment. The neurotic motivation pattern of hygiene seeking is mostly a learned process that arises from the value systems endemic in society.

Since total adaptation depends on the gratification of two separate types of needs, a rough operational categorization of adjustment can be made by examining the sources of a person's satisfactions.

A first category is characterized by positive mental health. Persons in this category show a preponderance of lifetime contentment stemming from situations in which the motivator factors are paramount. These factors are necessary in providing them with a sense of personal growth. They can be identified as directly involving the individual in some task, project or activity in which achievement or the consequences of achievement are possible. Those factors found meaningful for industrial job satisfaction may not be complete or may not be sufficiently descriptive to encompass the total life picture of an individual.

Other factors may be necessary to describe the motivators in this larger sense. Whatever they may be, the criteria for their selection must include activity on the part of the individual—some task, episode, adventure or activity in which the individual achieves a growth experience and without which the individual *will not* feel unhappy, dissatisfied or uncomfortable. In addition, to belong to this positive category the individual must have frequent opportunity for the gratification of these motivator needs. How frequent and how challenging the growth opportunities must be will depend on the level of ability (both genetic and learned) of the individual and, secondly, on his tolerance for delayed success. This tolerance, too, may be constitutional, learned or governed by dynamic conflicts; the source does not really matter to the argument.

The motivation-hygiene concept may seem to involve certain paradoxes. For example, is all achievement work and no play? Is the individual of limited ability doomed to be a nonachiever, and therefore a hygiene seeker?

In regard to work and play, achievements include all personal growth experiences. While it is true that *The Motivation to Work* focuses on industrial production, as demanded by society or company policy, the satisfying sequences reported are rich in examples of creativity and individual initiative. Artistic and scholarly interests, receptive openness to new insights, true relaxation and regrouping of growth potentials (as contrasted with plain laziness) are all achievement or elements in achievement. Nowhere is the balanced work-play growth element in achievement more apparent than in the mentally healthy individual.

In regard to limitations resulting from meager ability, the motivating history of achievement depends to an important degree on a realistic attitude. The individual who concerns himself largely with vague aspirations, completely unrelated to his abilities and to the actual situation, is simply one kind of hygiene seeker. He does not seek satisfaction in the job itself, but rather in those surrounding conditions that include such cultural noises as "any American boy can be president" or "every young man should have a college degree." The quotation by Carl Jung bears repetition: "The supreme goal of man is to fulfill himself as a creative, *unique* individual according to his own *innate potentialities* and within the *limits of reality.*" (Italics supplied.)

A final condition for membership in this mentally healthy group would be a good life environment or the successful avoidance of poor hygiene factors. Again, those conditions mentioned previously for the work situation may not suffice for all the environments of the individual.

Three conditions, then, will serve to define a mentally healthy individual: seeking life satisfaction through personal growth experiences (experiences defined as containing the motivator factors); sufficient success, commensurate with ability and tolerance for delay, to give direct evidence of growth, and, finally, successful avoidance of discomfort from poor hygiene.

If the hygiene is poor, the mental health is not affected, but obviously the individual becomes unhappy. This second category of adjustment-self-fulfillment, accompanied by dissatisfaction with the rewards of life, perhaps characterizes that large segment of the population that continues to do a good job despite reason for complaint. There is research evidence to support the idea that a motivator seeker who is effective in his performance will be listed among the gripers in a company. This is not surprising, for he feels justified in his criticisms because he earns his right to complain and is perhaps bright enough to see reasons for his ill temper.

A third category consists of individuals characterized by symptom-free adjustment. Individuals grouped in this category would also have sought and obtained their satisfactions primarily from the motivator factors. However, their growth needs will be much less reinforced during their life because of lack of opportunity. Such individuals will not have achieved a complete sense of accomplishment because of circumstances extrinsic to their motivation. Routine jobs and routine life experiences attenuate the growth of these individuals, not their motivation. Because their motivation is healthy, we do not place these persons on the sick continuum. In addition, those in this category must have sufficient satisfactions of their hygiene needs.

It is not unusual, though it is infrequent, to find that a respondent in the job-attitude investigations will stress one or more of the motivator factors as contributing to his job dissatisfaction. In other words, a satisfier acts as a dissatisfier. This occurrence most frequently includes the factors of failure of advancement, lack of recognition, lack of responsibility and uninteresting work. Closer inspection of these incidents reveals that many are insincere protestations covering a more latent hygiene desire. For example, the respondent who declares that his unhappiest time on the job occurred when his boss did not recognize his work is often saying that he misses the comfort and security of an accepting supervisor. His hygiene needs are simply wrapped in motivator clothing.

However, there are some highly growth-oriented persons who so desire the motivators and seek so very much a positive aspect for their lives that deprivation in this area may be interpreted by them as pain. In this case, their inversion of a motivator for a dissatisfaction episode is legitimate, but it represents a misinterpretation of their feelings. Their lack of happiness is felt as unhappiness, although it is qualitatively quite different from the unhappiness they experience because of the lack of the "hygiene" factors. Often these people summarize their job-attitude feelings by saying, "I really can't complain, but I sure don't like what I am doing," or, "As a job goes, this isn't bad, but I'm not getting anywhere."

The fourth category of essentially health-oriented people includes those who, paradoxically, are miserable. These are the motivator seekers who are denied any psychological growth opportunities and, in addition, find themselves with their hygiene needs simultaneously deprived. However miserable they might be, they are differentiated from the next three categories by their reluctance to adopt neurotic or psychotic defense mechanisms to allay their dual pain.

The next category represents a qualitative jump from the mental health dimension to the mental illness dimension. This category may be called the *maladjusted*. The basic characteristic of persons in this group is that they have sought positive satisfaction from the hygiene factors. There is an inversion of motivation away from the approach behavior of growth to the avoidance behavior of comfortable environments. Members of this group are the hygiene seekers, whose maladjustment is defined by the direction of their motivation and is evidenced by the environmental source of their satisfactions.

Many in this category will have had a significant number of personal achievements that result in no growth experience. It has been noted that hygiene satisfactions are short-lived and partake of the characteristics of opiates. The environmental satisfactions for persons whom we call maladjusted must be rather frequent and of substantial quality. It is the satisfactions of their hygiene needs that differentiate the maladjusted from the next category in our system—the mentally ill.

The mentally ill are lifetime hygiene seekers with poor hygiene satisfactions (as perceived by the individual). This poor hygiene may be realistic or it may reflect mostly the accentuated sensitivity to hygiene deprivation because of the inversion of motivation.

One of the extremes to which the "hygiene or maintenance" seeker resorts is to deny his hygiene needs altogether. This is termed the "monastic" defense. Seemingly, this line of reasoning asserts that the denial of man's animal nature will reward the individual with happiness, because the proponents of the "monastic" view of man's nature have discovered that no amount of hygiene rewards lead to human happiness. This sometime revered approach to the human dilemma now emerges as the blatant *non sequitur* that it is. How can psychological growth be achieved by denying hygiene realities? The illness is at two levels. The primary sickness is the denial of man's animal nature. Second, psychological growth and happiness depend on two separate factors, and no denial of irrelevant factors will serve man in his pursuit of happiness.

The motivation-hygiene concept holds that mental health depends on the individual's history or past experience. The history of the healthy individual shows success in growth achievements. In contrast, mental illness depends on a different pattern of past experience. The unhealthy individual has concerned himself with surrounding conditions. His search for satisfaction has focused on the limitations imposed by objective reality and by other individuals, including society and culture.

In the usual job situation these limitations consist of company policy, supervision, interpersonal relations and the like. In broader life adjustments the surrounding conditions include cultural taboos, social demands for material production and limited native ability. The hygiene seeker devotes his energies to concern with the surrounding limitations, to "defenses" in the Freudian sense. He seeks satisfaction, or mental health, in a policy of "defense." No personal growth occurs and his search for health is fruitless, for it leads to ever more intricate maneuvers of defense or hygiene seeking. Mental illness is an inversion—the attempt to accentuate or deny one set of needs in the hope of obtaining the other set.

To reiterate, mankind has two sets of needs. Think about man twice: once about events that cause him pain and, secondly, about events that make him happy. Those who seek only to gratify the needs of their animal natures are doomed to live in dreadful anticipation of pain and suffering. This is the fate of those human beings who want to satisfy only their biological needs. But some men have become aware of the advantage humans have over their animal brothers. In addition to the compulsion to avoid pain, the human being has been blessed with the potentiality to achieve happiness. And, as I hope I have demonstrated, man can be happy only by seeking to satisfy both his animal need to avoid pain and his human need to grow psychologically.

The seven classifications of adjustment continua are shown in Figure 2, using the motivation-hygiene theory frame of reference of parallel and diverging arrows. Within each category, the top arrow depicts the mental illness continuum and the bottom arrow the mental health continuum. The triangle signifies the scale on which the individual is operating and the degree of his gratification with the factors of that scale.

Category I: The healthy motivator seeker is shown to be on both the mental illness and the mental health continuua, and he is successful in achieving the motivator (mental health) needs and in avoiding the pain of the hygiene (mental illness) needs.

Category II: The unhappy motivator seeker is depicted as obtaining human significance from his job but receiving little amelioration of his animal-avoidance pains.

Category III: This shows the motivator seeker searching for

Figure 2

Adjustment Continua

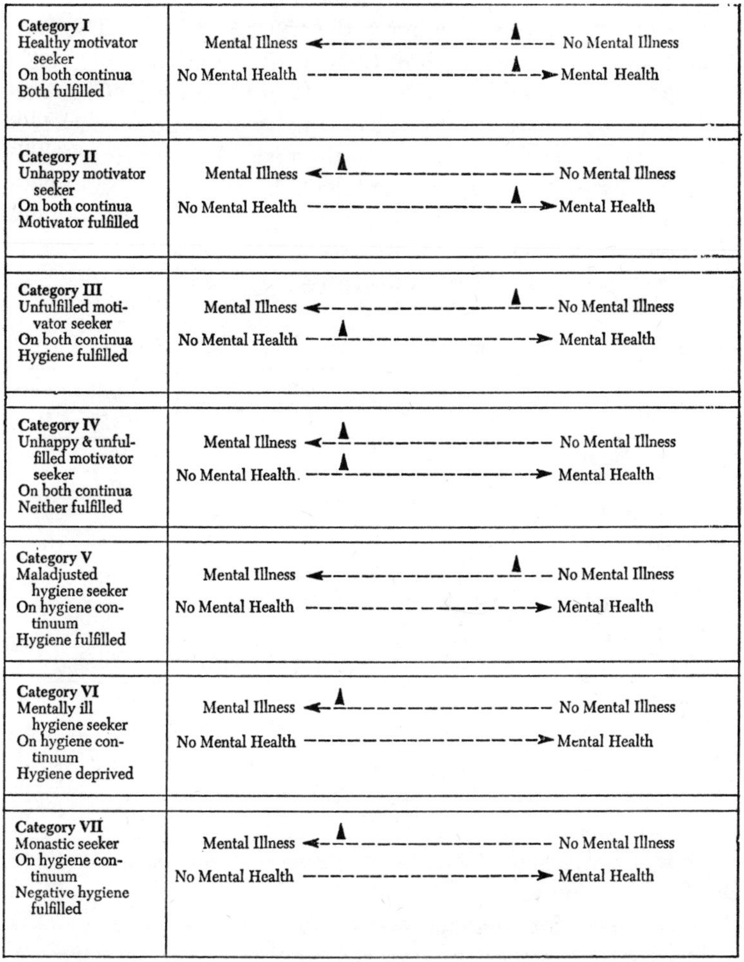

Category I Healthy motivator seeker On both continua Both fulfilled	Mental Illness ◄─ ─ ─ ─ ─ ─ ─ ─ ─ ─ ─ ─ ▲ ─ ─ ─ No Mental Illness No Mental Health ─ ─ ─ ─ ─ ─ ─ ─ ─ ─ ─ ─ ─ ▲ ─► Mental Health
Category II Unhappy motivator seeker On both continua Motivator fulfilled	Mental Illness ◄─ ▲ ─ ─ ─ ─ ─ ─ ─ ─ ─ ─ ─ No Mental Illness No Mental Health ─ ─ ─ ─ ─ ─ ─ ─ ─ ─ ─ ─ ▲ ─► Mental Health
Category III Unfulfilled moti- vator seeker On both continua Hygiene fulfilled	Mental Illness ◄─ ─ ─ ─ ─ ─ ─ ─ ─ ▲ ─ ─ No Mental Illness No Mental Health ─ ─ ─ ▲ ─ ─ ─ ─ ─ ─ ─ ─ ─ ─ ─► Mental Health
Category IV Unhappy & unful- filled motivator seeker On both continua Neither fulfilled	Mental Illness ◄─ ▲ ─ ─ ─ ─ ─ ─ ─ ─ ─ No Mental Illness No Mental Health. ─ ─ ▲ ─ ─ ─ ─ ─ ─ ─ ─ ─► Mental Health
Category V Maladjusted hygiene seeker On hygiene con- tinuum Hygiene fulfilled	Mental Illness ◄─ ─ ─ ─ ─ ─ ─ ─ ─ ▲ ─ ─ No Mental Illness No Mental Health ─ ─ ─ ─ ─ ─ ─ ─ ─ ─ ─► Mental Health
Category VI Mentally ill hygiene seeker On hygiene con- tinuum Hygiene deprived	Mental Illness ◄─ ▲ ─ ─ ─ ─ ─ ─ ─ ─ ─ No Mental Illness No Mental Health ─ ─ ─ ─ ─ ─ ─ ─ ─ ─ ─► Mental Health
Category VII Monastic seeker On hygiene con- tinuum Negative hygiene fulfilled	Mental Illness ◄─ ▲ ─ ─ ─ ─ ─ ─ ─ ─ ─ No Mental Illness No Mental Health ─ ─ ─ ─ ─ ─ ─ ─ ─ ─ ─► Mental Health

gratification of both sets of needs but being successful only in avoiding hygiene deprivation.

Category IV: The miserable motivator seeker is illustrated as basically healthy but, unfortunately, with neither need system being serviced.

Category V: The hygiene seeker who is motivated only by his hygiene needs is indicated here. He is successful at avoiding mental illness but debarred from achieving mental health.

Category VI: These people are the true mentally ill. They are the hygiene seekers who fail in their hygiene gratification.

Category VII: Finally, there is that interesting form of hygiene seeker, the "monastic," who also is living by only one need system and is fulfilling his hygiene requirements by denying them. Familiar examples are the no-talent beatnik, the sacrificing mother, the severe disciplinarian in the military world and, less often today, his counterpart in industry.

These types are summarized in Table I.

TABLE I   Types of Adjustments

Classification	Orientation	Motivator Satisfaction	Hygiene Satisfaction
Mental Health	Motivator	Yes	Yes
Unhappy	Motivator	Yes	No
Unfulfilled	Motivator	No	Yes
Unhappy and unfulfilled	Motivator	No	No
Maladjusted	Hygiene	Not pertinent	Yes
Mental illness	Hygiene	Not pertinent	No
Monastic	Hygiene	Not pertinent	Denied

Can we identify the people on jobs who are the healthy individuals, that is, who are the motivator seekers, as distinguished from the hygiene seekers? What are the consequences to companies that select and reinforce hygiene seekers? These questions will be examined in the final chapter, but at this point a brief description of hygiene seekers and of the consequences to the company hiring them will be useful.

The hygiene seeker, as opposed to the motivator seeker, is motivated by the nature of the environment of his job rather than by his tasks. He suffers from a chronic and heightened dissatisfaction with his job hygiene. Why? Because he lives by it. He has an overreaction to improvement in hygiene factors. You give him a salary raise and you become the most wonderful boss in the world; he is in the most wonderful company in the world—he protests too much. In other words, you have given him a shot in the arm. But the satisfactions of hygiene factors are of short duration—and the short action applies as well to the motivator seeker, because this is the nature of the beast.

The hygiene seeker realizes little satisfaction from accomplishments and consequently shows little interest in the kind and quality of the work he does. Why? Since he is basically an avoidance-oriented organism, how can he have a positive outlook on life? He does not profit professionally from experience. The only profit he desires is a more comfortable environment. "What did you learn?" "Nothing, it was a complete waste of time." Obviously, there was no definite reward. In other words, even though you can stimulate him for a temporary action, he does not have his own generator. And I think, also, that many companies feel they have to keep doing his stimulating.

The hygiene seeker is ultraliberal or ultraconservative. He parrots management's philosophy. As a means of reducing ambiguity he acts more like top management than top management does. The question arises whether he may be successful on the job because of talent. The question is then legitimately asked: If a man does well on the job because of hygiene satisfactions, what difference does it make?

The answer is twofold. I believe that hygiene seekers will let the company down when their talents are most needed. They are motivated only for short times and only when there is an external reward to be obtained. It is just when an emergency situation arises, and when the organization cannot be bothered with hygiene, that these key men may fail to do their jobs. In the Army, they are known as "barracks soldiers."

The second answer I suggest, and one that I believe to be of more serious import, is that hygiene seekers offer their own motivational characteristics as the pattern to be instilled in their subordinates. They become the template from which the new recruit to industry learns his motivational pattern. Hygiene seekers in key positions set the extrinsic reward atmosphere for the units of the company that they control. Because of the talent they possess, their influence on conditioning the atmosphere is generally out of proportion to their long-term effectiveness to the company.

TABLE II   Characteristics of Hygiene and Motivation Seekers

Hygiene Seeker	Motivation Seeker
1. Motivated by nature of the environment	Motivated by nature of the task
2. Chronic and heightened dissatisfaction with various aspects of his job context, e. g., salary, supervision, working conditions, status, job security, company policy and administration, fellow employees	Higher tolerance for poor hygiene factors
3. Overreaction with satisfaction to improvement in hygiene factors	Less reaction to improvement in hygiene factors
4. Short duration of satisfaction when the hygiene factors are improved	Similar
5. Overreaction with dissatisfaction when hygiene factors are not improved	Milder discontent when hygiene factors need improvement
6. Realizes little satisfactions from accomplishments	Realizes great satisfaction from accomplishments
7. Shows little interest in the kind and quality of the work he does	Shows capacity to enjoy the kind of work he does
8. Cynicism regarding positive virtues of work and life in general	Has positive feelings toward work and life in general
9. Does not profit professionally from experience	Profits professionally from experience
10. Prone to cultural noises a. Ultraliberal, ultraconservative b. Parrots management philosophy c. Acts more like top management than top management does	Belief systems sincere and considered
11. May be successful on the job because of talent	May be an overachiever

If we accept the notion that one of the most important functions of a manager is the development of future managers, the teaching of hygiene motivations becomes a serious defect to the company. This, I believe, is one of the major implications that the motivation-hygiene theory has for modern personnel practices. Previous research knowledge has strongly indicated that the effectiveness of management development is attuned to its congruence with the company atmosphere, as it is manifested in the superior's beliefs and behavior. The superior who is a hygiene seeker cannot but have an adverse effect on management development, which is aimed at the personal growth and actualization of subordinates.

Table II summarizes the characteristics of the hygiene seeker and the motivator seeker as manifested at work. Further explorations of their characteristics will be made in the final chapter.

In this chapter, we have given a brief summary of the motivation-hygiene theory, which began with a study of job attitudes of engineers and accountants in Pittsburgh. In the next two chapters, the subsequent investigations that document this theory will be reviewed.

7

Verification of the Theory
of Motivation-Hygiene

THE ORIGINAL STUDY of job attitudes, published in *The Motivation to Work*, has received wide acceptance and some justified criticism. One of the most pertinent of the criticisms concerns the overgeneralization of the theory because the evidence was based on a restricted sample of accountants and engineers. Another related and valid criticism centers on the very nature of psychological investigations. Because of the unreliability of many of its findings, psychological research is more suspect than research in the hard sciences. This unreliability stems largely from the number of variables involved and also from the more subtle intrusion of the bias of the investigator. More than in any other science, replication of research is a must in psychology, in order to substantiate findings. *The Motivation to Work* was one study, by one set of investigators, and therefore its conclusions should be considered tentative until independent verification is offered.

One of the most gratifying consequences of the publication of *The Motivation to Work* has been the large number of investigations that it has engendered and that were designed to test its basic validity, the degree to which it can be generalized to other populations and its applicability to industrial as well as mental health problems. In subsequent sections, these follow-up studies are reviewed.

Perhaps the most significant attempt to verify the original findings is a direct reproduction of the research pattern, but with the use of a wider range of occupations and under the direction of different investigators. At the time of this writing, nine such repetitions of the initial work have been reported, increasing the number of different occupations to a total of seventeen, representing the widest range of skills, job levels and types of organizations. In addition, two projects include cross-cultural samples of employees working in Finnish and Hungarian industry. A project to include workers in the Soviet Union has not been completed in time to be included in this report.

Each of these inquiries into job attitudes uses approximately the same format, including the interview questions, the method of analysis and the job factors into which the responses were coded. The common pattern interview is reproduced below:

Think of a time when you felt exceptionally good or exceptionally bad about your present job or any other job you have had. Tell me what happened.

1. How long ago did this happen?
2. How long did the feeling last? Can you describe specifically what made the change of feelings begin? When did it end?
3. Was what happened typical of what was going on at the time?
4. Can you tell more precisely why you felt the way you did at the time?
5. What did these events mean to you?
6. Did these feelings affect the way you did your job? How? How long did this go on?
7. Can you give a specific example of the way in which your performance on the job was affected? For how long?
8. Did what happened affect you personally in any way? For how long? Did it change the way you got along with people in general or with your family? Did it affect your sleep, appetite, digestion, general health?
9. Did what happened basically affect the way you felt

about working at that company or did it merely make you feel good or bad about the occurrence itself?

10. Did the consequences of what happened at this time affect your career? How?

11. Did what happened change the way you felt about your profession? How?

12. How seriously were your feelings (good or bad) about your job affected by what happened? Pick a spot on the line below to indicate how strong you think the good or bad feelings were. Circle that position on the line.

Least	Average	Greatest
1 2 3 4 5 6 7 8 9 10 11 12 13 14 15 16 17 18 19 20 21		

Note: Number 1 should be used for a sequence that hardly affected your feelings; 21 should be used for a sequence that affected your feelings as seriously as the most important events in your working experience.

13. Could the situation you described happen again for the same reasons and with the same effects? If not, describe the changes that have taken place which would make your feelings and actions different today from what they were then.

14. Is there anything else you would like to say about the sequence of events you have described?

After the subject is asked the preceding questions, he is then asked the same follow-up question for the second sequence of events: "Now that you have described a time when you felt exceptionally good or exceptionally bad about your job, please think of another time, one during which you felt exceptionally good or exceptionally bad about your job."

A brief comment on this methodology may serve to explain why it was chosen. Attitude research in psychology has a long and tortuous history. The definition of what an attitude is and how it differs from similar concepts (such as opinions, interests, feelings and tendencies) have never been satisfactorily resolved. Further, how can one know when someone has an attitude or a feeling about something? Experience with attitude and opinion surveys is replete with evidence that people are prone to give responses indicating a position or even strong feelings regarding a matter about which, in fact, they couldn't care less. Frequently, responses are given without the faintest idea of what the interviewer wants or what the questionnaire is about. People are likely to respond simply to participate, and in these instances they often provide answers that are mostly cultural noises for their particular reference groups, answers that are ego-enhancing and other answers that are quite irrelevant. Decades of research and development in constructing scales for the measurement of job attitudes have mostly revealed information about the scales and discouragingly little about job attitudes per se.

The rationale of the "sequence of events method" is to assure the investigator that a real attitude exists by studying the change in attitudes. Selecting periods of time when the respondent felt exceptionally good or bad suggests that he was feeling different from the way he had felt before. If he is feeling different, there is more likelihood that an attitude or feeling is being tapped. Focusing on specific events also gives greater assurance that the respondent was personally involved. In this way the investigator, by analyzing the nature of the events themselves, can avoid much of the rationalizations and other beclouders of the respondent's explanations. These events are the basic information for the research. They are coded into factors that are essentially shorthand notations of what was going on during the period of these exceptional feelings. For more details on the methods, see *The Motivation to Work.*

The first-level factors examined totaled sixteen, six motivators and ten hygiene or maintenance factors. The motivators are:

1. Achievement
2. Recognition for achievement
3. Work itself
4. Responsibility
5. Advancement
6. Possibility of growth

The hygiene factors are:

1. Supervision
2. Company policy and administration
3. Working conditions

4–6. Interpersonal relations with peers, subordinates and superiors

7. Status
8. Job security
9. Salary
10. Personal life

The definition of each factor will be found in the appendix. In the original study, and in many of the replications, a second level of analysis was made of the events. The respondents were asked, as part of the interview, to explain why the particular happenings they had described affected them as they did. The following second-level factors were used to catalogue the psychological reactions of the employees to the events:

1. Achievement
2. Possible growth
3. Advancement
4. Responsibility
5. Group feeling
6. Work itself
7. Status
8. Security
9. Feelings of fairness or unfairness
10. Feelings of pride or shame
11. Salary

It should be emphasized that the more objective first-level analysis of the events takes precedence over the more subjective second-level analysis.

The specific findings for each of the populations are charted in the same way in the following seventeen diagrams, beginning with the diagrams of the initial study shown in the previous chapter. The results for engineers and accountants are portrayed separately in figures 3 and 4. Accompanying each diagram, except for the first two, which have already been reviewed, is a commentary on the results and on any differences in the methodology of the investigation.

The first replication of the original research to be published was the project by Dr. Milton M. Schwartz and his colleagues at Rutgers University. The authors' stated purpose was to "check on the results previously obtained but with a different population,

Figure 3

Comparison of Satisfiers and Dissatisfiers

Pittsburgh Engineers

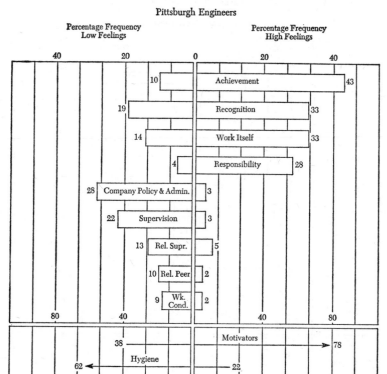

Data from F. Herzberg *et al.*

specifically those with supervisor responsibilities in nonprofessional occupations." As indicated before, the generalization of the meaning of the motivation to work theory was possibly restricted because of the limited range of jobs that characterized the initial population. In addition, the Schwartz group felt that the lack of supervisory functions of the original population was an especially important variable to investigate.

Their subjects consisted of 111 male supervisors, distributed among 21 electric and gas utility companies of the Middle Atlantic and New England states, who were enrolled in a management-training program at the Rutgers University extension

Figure 4

Comparison of Satisfiers and Dissatisfiers

Pittsburgh Accountants

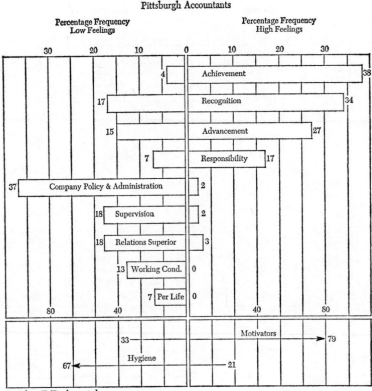

Data from F. Herzberg *et al.*

division during 1960 and 1961. Their ages ranged from 27 to 62 years, with a mean of 40 years. In contrast to the original population of engineers and accountants, only 31 of these subjects were college graduates, although about half of the group had some college education.

The persons in the Schwartz study were limited to the lower half of the managerial hierarchy, although they did represent all activities of utility operations. The authors characterized their population as long-tenured employees in "an industry noted for low personnel turnover and a high security and stability emphasis." The authors further suggest that there was "a remarkable degree of situation homogeneity," which they feel largely eliminated the intrusion of situational variables affecting their results.

Two changes in methodology should be noted. First, rather than interview their subjects, the Schwartz group resorted to a questionnaire patterned after the interview. Originally, this questionnaire was used by the present author during his pilot investigations leading to the major study. The other change was in the analysis of the incidents or sequences of events, Schwartz and his associates limiting themselves to the first-level factors (i.e., the objective events) without going into the psychological significance that the events had for the respondents. The authors state that "no serious loss was felt to derive from these changes, as our intent was to keep the method as direct and as objective as possible without fundamentally altering the original experiment."

The findings of this research are highly corroborative of the motivation to work theory as shown in the results portrayed in Figure 5. At the bottom of the chart, the frequency of the motivators during high job-attitude feelings and low job-attitude feelings is contrasted with the frequency of the hygiene factors during these opposite states of affect. The motivators favor the satisfaction sequences by more than a 7-to-1 ratio, while the hygiene factors relate to the dissatisfaction sequences by a ratio of approximately 3 to 2. The differences portrayed here, as in all charts to follow, are statistically significant.

With respect to the specific factors that were involved in producing high and low feelings on the job, only one factor showed a significant reversal from the predicted direction—*interpersonal relationships with the subordinates*. In this instance, a hygiene factor was found to occur significantly more often in positive job-attitude sequences than in negative job-attitude sequences, contrary to the expectations of the theory.

Of the six motivators (*achievement, recognition, work itself, responsibility, advancement* and *possibility of growth*), all but *work itself* occurred more frequently in the high job-attitude sequences than in low attitude sequences. Thus it appears that the motivator factors in the Schwartz studies emphatically verified the results of the pioneer research.

Of the ten hygiene factors derived from the original work, these

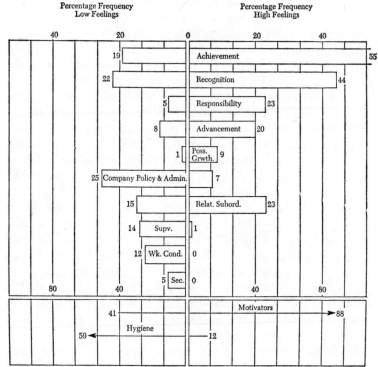

Figure 5

Comparison of Satisfiers and Dissatisfiers

Lower-Level Supervisors in Utility Industry

Data from M. Schwartz et al.

were also reported by Schwartz to be significantly more frequent in the low job-attitude sequences: *company policy and administration, interpersonal relationships with subordinates, supervision, working conditions* and *security.* The hygiene factors, with the sole exception of *interpersonal relationships with subordinates* previously noted, also appear to be very much verified. Commentary on this single exception will be included in the over-all analysis to be made after all the investigations have been presented.

Another worthwhile agreement between the Schwartz and Herzberg studies was the finding that there were no variations in the results when they were analyzed for differences in age, job classifications, education or personality characteristics. Similar findings of minimal differences in the basic results for various characteristics of the subjects are reported in *The Motivation to Work*.

The second duplication is based on another sample of lower-level supervisors, but this time representing a wide range of industries in Finland. This study was carried out while the writer was spending a sabbatical year at the Yhteiskunnallisen Korkea-koulun in Tampere, Finland. The study was sponsored by the Research Institute at the School of Social Science in Tampere and by the Institute of Industrial Supervision in Helsinki. The 139 subjects of this investigation, with an age range of from 23 to 62 years (with a mean of 36), were given a translated version of the same questionnaire that Schwartz had used. They completed the questionnaire during the time they were participating in managerial-development conferences at the Institute of Industrial Supervision. Thus, the author was able to obtain a wide cross-section of Finnish industry, inasmuch as this course attracted persons from all companies in that country. A pilot study with engineers in three companies in the city of Tampere had previously served to verify the adequacy of the translation and to smooth out the other difficulties inherent in cross-cultural investigations.

The results are shown in Figure 6. Since the Finnish study was conducted by the author of the theory, the results were verified by an independent analysis by Dr. Robert Lee, formerly of Western Reserve University.

Once again, the two arrows shown at the bottom of the chart, indicating the divergent trends for motivators and hygiene factors, serve to verify the basic theory as these factors are involved in positive and negative job-attitude sequences.

With respect to the factors themselves, five of the six motivators are found to be significantly unidirectional; the only one not appearing more frequently in the high- versus the low-feeling sequences was *possibility of growth*, and this occurred with the original study.

Four hygiene factors appear with significantly greater frequency in the low sequences than in the high ones—*supervision,*

Figure 6

Comparison of Satisfiers and Dissatisfiers

Finnish Supervisors

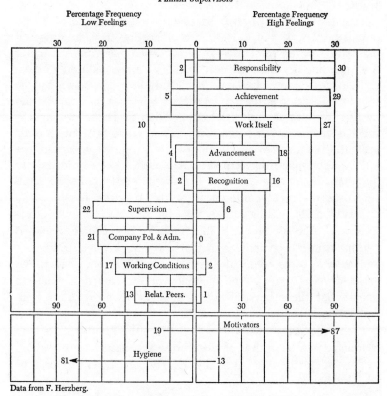

Data from F. Herzberg.

company policy and administration, working conditions and *interpersonal relationships with peers.* No inversions of the factors occurred, i. e., a motivator was never found more frequently in the low sequences than in the high, nor was a hygiene need more frequently found for the positive attitudes. Our analysis of the effect of age and education on these results once again revealed no meaningful alterations in the findings. This study with Finnish managers is thus confirmatory of the basic thesis presented.

Professional women were the subjects investigated in another identical replication of *The Motivation to Work* undertaken by

Dr. Elizabeth Walt of the American University. Fifty women employed by United States government installations involved in research and analytical work in economics, languages, mathematics and engineering, on a high professional level, were interviewed by the procedure of eliciting a sequence of events. The subjects averaged 45 years in age, with a range from the early 30s to the 60s. Their education was quite advanced, as might be expected from their high-level jobs; nearly half had earned graduate degrees. This is the first investigation using women as subjects to be reported. It will be interesting to contrast highly trained professional women with women doing routine jobs in another investigation at the Texas Instruments Company, described later.

Inasmuch as Dr. Walt made an exact replication of the original study, the results can be presented quickly. The over-all validity of the theory regarding the job attitude of women is once again shown by the two diverging arrows at the bottom of Figure 7.

Four of the motivators, *achievement, work itself, responsibility* and *recognition,* in that order of frequency, appeared significantly more often when job satisfaction events were listed. *Advancement* and *possibility of growth* were the two motivators that failed to discriminate this time.

Among the hygiene factors, the ubiquitous *company policy and administration* was once again the most frequent source of job unhappiness. Three additional hygiene factors operated in the predicted negative fashion; they were *status, working conditions* and factors in their *personal lives. Supervision* did not show a significant difference, while *job security* and *salary* were only minimally mentioned. The two remaining hygiene factors—*interpersonal relationships with peers* and *interpersonal relationships with subordinates*—while not occurring with any great frequency, were nevertheless found significantly more often in high job-attitude sequences than in low sequences. It should be noted that the only other failure of a factor to operate in the predicted direction was also that of *interpersonal relationships* in the Rutgers study. These two inversions are the only failures in predictions to be found in all the studies reported.

The second-level analysis of the factors, i.e., an analysis of the meaning the events had for the respondents, once again showed

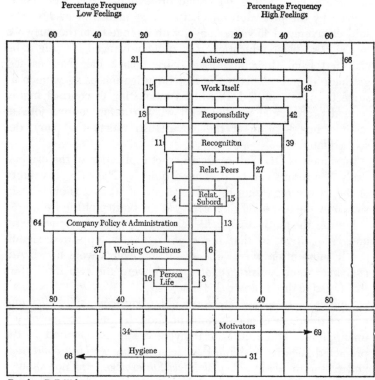

Figure 7

Comparison of Satisfiers and Dissatisfiers

Women in High-Level Professional Positions

Data from D. E. Walt.

what was reported in the original study—that the basis for satisfaction lay in the individual's accomplishment, while the basis for her dissatisfaction stemmed from her perception of the unfairness in the environment. Walt also duplicated many of the other analyses appearing in *The Motivation to Work*, with similar confirmations, particularly those dealing with the interrelationships of the factors and the effects that the incidents had on various performance measures. The reader is referred to *The Motivation to Work* for these aspects of the studies.

Another complete replication of the original experiment was

carried out by Dr. Denzil Clegg. This time a population of 58 county administrators of the cooperative extension service in agriculture at the University of Nebraska was used. A chief interest in this investigation was to determine if the motivation-hygiene dichotomy in job attitudes would apply to personnel who were not housed in a central company location, but were dispersed in offices over an entire state. All the people studied were college graduates with at least two years of work experience. Their tenure averaged 12 years, and the mean age was about 40 years.

Clegg introduced a minor variation in the research method. In order to assure the collection of the really important events from his respondents, he required that he be provided with three positive and three negative incidents. Then the respondents were asked to rank these incidents in order of importance. Clegg chose the most important one of each set of three for his analysis. The same sixteen factors were used with the addition of two new ones, unique to the job of these supervisors—*interpersonal relationships with clientele* and *relationships with members of the extension board*, both hygiene factors.

The results are shown in Figure 8. Once again, the over-all theory is verified by the divergent arrows at the bottom of the chart. With respect to the specific factors, two of the motivators—*achievement* and *recognition*—are significantly in the predicted direction of satisfaction, while six of the ten hygiene factors are significantly related to dissatisfaction. These latter six are *company policy and administration, working conditions, interpersonal relationships with subordinates and with peers, supervision* and *personal life.* One of the two added hygiene factors, *relationships with the extension board,* was also significant in bringing about dissatisfaction.

Clegg was able to verify the findings at the second-level analysis (psychological meaning) of the events when he reported that the major reasons given by his subjects for their feelings of satisfaction were the need for achievement and recognition, while the feelings of dissatisfaction were engendered by perceived unfair treatment at work. The effects of the attitudes on performance, turnover and morale were also in line with those found in previous studies (Herzberg *et al.* and Walt.)

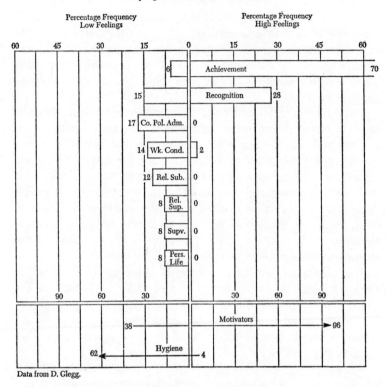

Figure 8

Comparison of Satisfiers and Dissatisfiers

County Agriculture Extension Workers

Data from D. Clegg.

The next experiment to be examined was based on an unusual population: pre-retirees from managerial positions in a variety of Cleveland industries. The major objective of this doctoral dissertation by Shoukry Saleh was to demonstrate the two-factor theory with an older population, who were a few years away from the end of their formal working life. An additional objective, to be reported on later, was to predict attitudes toward retirement between those with a "hygiene-seeking" attitude to work and those oriented toward "motivator seeking."

The subjects were 85 managerial employees between the ages

of 60 and 65, drawn from 12 Cleveland companies with compulsory retirement at age 65. The companies included three utilities, a bank, and eight manufacturing concerns making chemical, oil, steel and electrical products.

Once again, the basic motivation-hygiene interview was used to obtain sequences of the events in which each respondent described a happy job experience and recalled an event related to an unhappy job experience. Since each subject was near retirement, the sampling of incidents spanned a lifetime of work, although the majority who reported ranged from 40 to 60 years.

The same 16 job factors and the same method for analyzing and coding the interviews, developed in the original study and utilized by all replications, were also used by Saleh. With the exception of limiting the respondent to only one "high" and one "low" sequence, this part of the study is an exact duplicate of the original.

The results shown in Figure 9 indicate that the same five of the six motivators that the original project found significantly more often among the satisfaction sequences were also significant in the same direction in the Saleh investigation. *Possibility of growth* was the motivator that failed to differentiate satisfier from dissatisfier events.

The hygiene factors were the only factors found significantly more often among the dissatisfaction sequences. Those that were statistically significant included the perennial *company policy and administration, supervision, interpersonal relationships with peers* and *interpersonal relationships with subordinates.* The other five hygiene factors (*salary, working conditions, personal life, status* and *job security*), although in each instance more frequent in the low sequences, were not significantly so.

The diverging arrows at the bottom of the chart confirm the theory; 89 per cent of the positive-attitude sequences involved the motivators, in contrast to only 33 per cent for the negative-attitude events. Hygiene factors, on the other hand, were six times as frequent in causing negative job attitudes as they were in bringing about positive feelings.

The second-level analysis generally paralleled the previous results—achievement and growth needs for the satisfaction re-

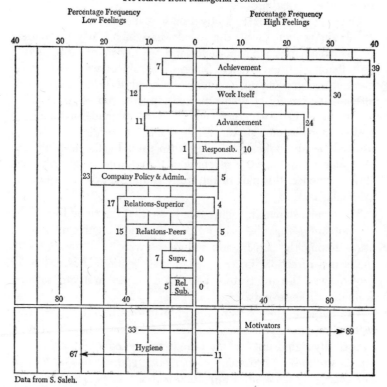

Figure 9

Comparison of Satisfiers and Dissatisfiers

Pre-retirees from Managerial Positions

Data from S. Saleh.

sponses, and objection to perceived unfair treatment for the dissatisfaction responses.

The Saleh study provides for an extreme generalization of the theory by emphasizing the importance of the motivators to job satisfaction even among those who are about to retire from formal work.

An article entitled "Who Are Your Motivated Workers," by M. Scott Myers in the *Harvard Business Review* (January-February, 1964), summarized the results of a replication of *The Motivation to Work* that had been carried out as part of a new orientation to industrial relations at the Texas Instruments Company of Dallas. This inquiry is of interest not only because of its verification of the basic theory but also because it has been utilized as a means of bringing the implications of the theory into active management thinking and practice.

The population of the study consisted of 282 employees of the Texas Instruments Company's installations at Dallas. Included in the 282 were 50 scientists, 55 engineers, 50 manufacturing supervisors, 75 male technicians and 52 female hourly assemblers. Once again, the methodology was almost a precise replica of the original investigation. There was one important variation in the tabulation of the results of the interviews. Myers coded only one factor per sequence of events, the one he considered to be the most important, thereby reducing the number of factors that could manifest themselves in the count. For example, 44 per cent of all the satisfaction events were coded with the *achievement* factor, thus leaving slightly more than half the events to be distributed among the other 13 factors Herzberg used. Two of the original factors, *interpersonal relations with subordinates* and *personal life*, were for unknown reasons not utilized by Myers. In all other studies, as many factors as were necessary to describe the events were coded, and thus the frequency of any one factor was not limited by any other. This latter procedure is viewed by the writer as a better one, because it more adequately summarizes the events and also eliminates the questionable judgment of the coder when he attempts to decide which is the major factor in the incident. However, the important point to remember when viewing the results is that few factors can appear with significantly different frequences between the high and low job-attitude events. Those that do should, however, be in the hypothesized direction.

Since one of the basic objectives of this review is to show the wide generality of populations for which the theory holds, the results are shown separately for each of the five occupations at Texas Instruments.

Figure 10 presents the results for the 50 scientists. The diverging arrows indicate that the events describing periods of job satisfaction were overwhelmingly brought about by one or more

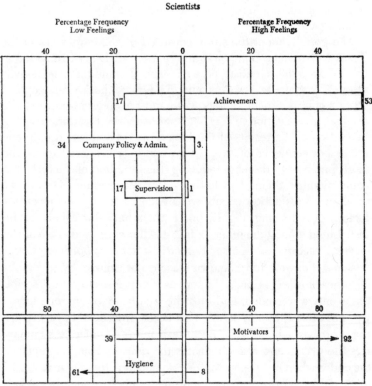

Figure 10

Comparison of Satisfiers and Dissatisfiers

Scientists

Data from M. S. Myers.

of the motivator factors. The hygiene factors, on the other hand, appear twice as often as instruments for job dissatisfaction than do the motivators.

For three of the factors, there is a statistically significant difference in the frequency between high and low job-attitude events. As indicated above, the method of analysis limits the number of factors that can manifest such differences. The most common motivator, *achievement,* and the two most frequent hygiene factors, *company policy and administration* and *supervision,* are all in the predicted direction.

The results for another sample of engineers (engineers, the reader will recall, made up half the population of the Herzberg study) are given in Figure 11. The results are identical with those for the scientists.

Figure 11

Comparison of Satisfiers and Dissatisfiers

Engineers

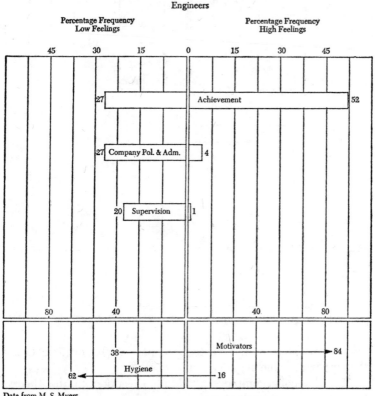

Data from M. S. Myers.

Figure 12 contains the findings for manufacturing supervisors. The diverging arrows are as predicted, and so are the three factors that showed significant differences between high and low job-attitude events. This time *recognition* joins its fellow motivator, *achievement*. For the negative events, *company policy and*

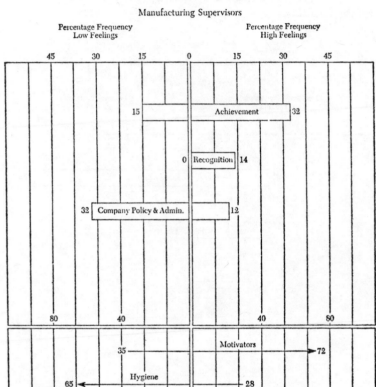

Figure 12

Comparison of Satisfiers and Dissatisfiers

Manufacturing Supervisors

Data from M. S. Myers.

administration is, as is now to be expected, the hygiene factor that appears for the negative sequences.

The blue-collar employees are no exception to the theory. Contrary to what most of us have been led to believe, the rank-and-file worker has no basic needs that are different from those of his colleagues with white shirts. I will comment further on this in the concluding chapter.

The results for the 75 male hourly technicians are given in Figure 13. The diverging arrows are there; so are three motivators (*achievement, recognition* and *responsibility*) and two

Figure 13

Comparison of Satisfiers and Dissatisfiers

Male Hourly Technicians

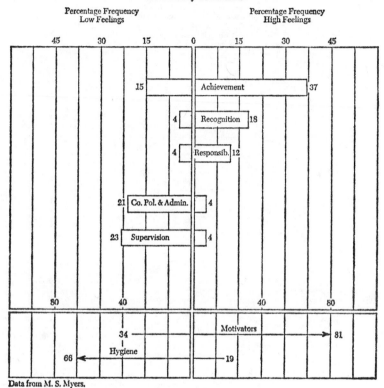

Percentage Frequency
Low Feelings

Percentage Frequency
High Feelings

Data from M. S. Myers.

hygiene factors (*company policy and administration* and *supervision*), all significantly in the predicted direction.

Finally, the theory holds for the most unlikely group, female assemblers. Again, contrary to all past thinking and research on women employed in routine jobs to the effect that they are primarily concerned with the work environment, their overriding source of job satisfaction is shown to be *achievement,* followed by *recognition.* While no hygiene factor was found to be significant, the diverging arrows verify the theory for these women when all the factors are considered. Figure 14 contains the results for the female assemblers.

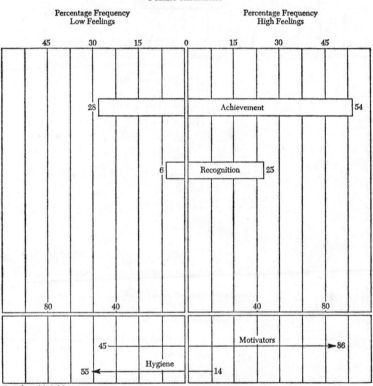

Figure 14

Comparison of Satisfiers and Dissatisfiers

Female Assemblers

Data from M. S. Myers.

In summary, the Texas Instruments Company's research, with five varied occupations from scientists to female assemblers, confirms the basic theory.

The next two replications to be reported offer a considerable broadening of the level of the job and of the type of organization to which the theory applies. Both replications were conducted in Veterans Administration hospitals, the first in Utah and the second in two Veterans Administration installations in Cleveland, Ohio.

The Utah research was conducted by Dr. Frederick Anderson, who included in his study 29 professional nurses, a "skilled" group of 31 workers employed in engineering maintenance services, and an "unskilled" group of 35 workers engaged in food services and routine engineering services. Because of the low occupational level of most of his subjects, but, more important, owing to problems in the interviewing situation, approximately one-third of the workers interviewed could not think of a period in their work history when they had exceptionally good feelings. The result of this inability to obtain sequences, combined with the initial small numbers investigated, limited the chances for finding significant differences among the factors. Accordingly, some of the factors in the three charts portraying the data of this study are drawn with broken lines to indicate that these factors fell short of statistical significance; but had the number been slightly larger, these factors would have differentiated between high and low job attitudes at a level of acceptable statistical significance. With this limitation in interpreting the findings, the following three charts summarize Anderson's findings.

The professional nurses are described in Figure 15. For all the events taken together, the motivators appear in the high job-attitude sequences approximately three times as often as do the hygiene factors, and the hygiene factors appear twice as often in the negative attitude events than do the motivators.

Five factors for the sample of nurses show or approach statistical significance in their association with positive or negative job attitudes. For the positive events there are the two motivators, *recognition* and *achievement,* and for the negative sequences three hygiene factors, *company policy and administration, interpersonal relationships with superiors* and *working conditions.*

The results for the second sample of the Anderson study, the skilled maintenance employees, are given in Figure 16. Three motivators, *recognition, achievement* and *possibility of growth,* are found more frequently in the high incidents, while the hygiene factors of *company policy and administration* and *supervision* appear more frequently in the low incidents. For all factors

Figure 15

Comparison of Satisfiers and Dissatisfiers

Hospital Nurses

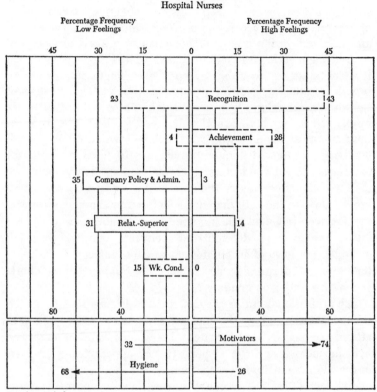

Data from F. Anderson.

combined, shown by the diverging arrows, the hygiene factors are overwhelmingly associated with the dissatisfaction events, although this time the motivators are not so one-sided in their association with the events describing periods of job satisfaction.

The third of Anderson's sample is very intriguing, for the service employees represent the lowest levels of the occupational and educational ladder yet examined. However, as depicted in Figure 17, the theory still holds rather well. The divergence of the arrows is more pronounced than for the previous population, thus supporting the motivation-hygiene concept when all the events

Figure 16

Comparison of Satisfiers and Dissatisfiers

Skilled Hospital Employees

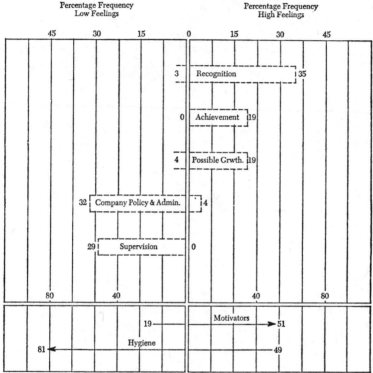

Data from F. Anderson.

are considered. With respect to the factors themselves, the motivators *recognition* and *responsibility* approach significance as differentiating satisfaction from dissatisfaction, and the three hygiene factors of *company policy and administration, supervision* and *interpersonal relations with peers* are similarly related to the events describing job dissatisfactions.

The next replication to be cited is another doctoral dissertation by Howard Gendel (Western Reserve University, 1965), whose purpose was to confirm the theory as it applied to the low-level jobs for which Anderson's study provided only tentative

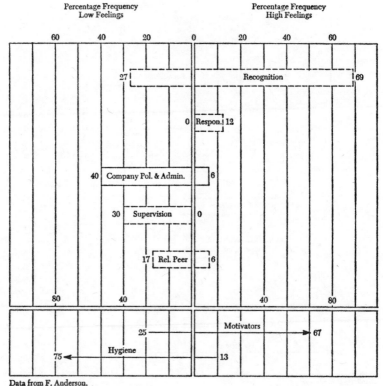

Figure 17

Comparison of Satisfiers and Dissatisfiers

Unskilled Hospital Employees

Data from F. Anderson.

support. In this instance, the subjects were 119 housekeeping workers at two Veterans Administration hospitals in Cleveland. An increase in the size of the sample and a review of the interviewing methods with the present writer led to solid statistical evidence of the theory. It should be added that more than 90 per cent of the housekeepers were Negroes. While the race of the group should be irrelevant, it is mentioned to dispel aspersions that are commonly cast on Negroes' achievement motivation.

Figure 18 presents the evidence. The motivators are found with a 4-to-1 majority in the high sequences, while the hygiene factors

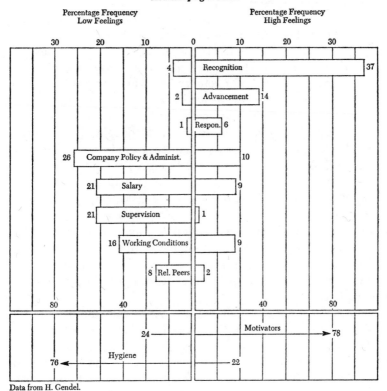

Figure 18

Comparison of Satisfiers and Dissatisfiers

Housekeeping Workers

Data from H. Gendel.

are shown to be associated with the low sequences in a more than 3-to-1 ratio.

The motivators that were significant are *recognition, advancement* and *responsibility*. An interesting result for the hygiene factors occurred. For the first time in any study, *salary* appears significant as a dissatisfier, which according to the theory and to other evidence it should be. Four other hygiene factors were significant as dissatisfiers: *working conditions, interpersonal relationships with peers* and, of course, *company policy and administration* and *supervision*.

Gendel also confirmed the findings of the original study and other replications (Walt, Clegg, Saleh) with respect to the second-level responses and the effect the attitudes had on various performance and personal criteria.

The ninth and last replication of the original investigation to be included in this part of the review comes from a recent study completed by Dr. J. Perczel of the Ganz Mavag Locomotive Works in Budapest, Hungary. I had been anxious to obtain a sample from a Communist country and had expected to be able to report on the research being conducted in Leningrad. This past summer, I received an invitation to lecture in Budapest to the Society of Engineers and found, to my delight, that a motivation-hygiene study was being made on a group of engineers by the psychologist for Ganz Mavag. The complete data is not available at the time of this writing, but Figure 19, given to me by Dr. Perczel, is highly supportive of the basic theory. The motivators *work itself, achievement, recognition* and *responsibility* and the hygiene factors *company policy and administration* and *supervision* are all statistically significant in the predicted direction. Evidently the motivation-hygiene theory is as relevant to different economic and political systems as it is to types of occupations.

In the next chapter, a description of the first empirical morale survey ever performed in the Soviet Union will be presented. In that survey, the Russian investigators suggest that the Communist worker is motivated by the motivators, while the workers in a capitalist society are primarily wrapped up with hygiene concerns. In the January, 1965, issue of the official Russian publication in America, *Soviet Life,* Professor Vladimir Yadov of the University of Leningrad pursues this view by challenging my critical comments on his conclusions, in the *New York Times.* Joint research between this author and Professor Yadov is currently under way to submit the argument to a direct test. In the meantime, the Hungarian study seems to be evidence that the pattern of job attitudes in one Communist society is no different from that in the Western nations.

A summary of the findings on the 17 populations, for which essentially the same methods were used, is given in the following

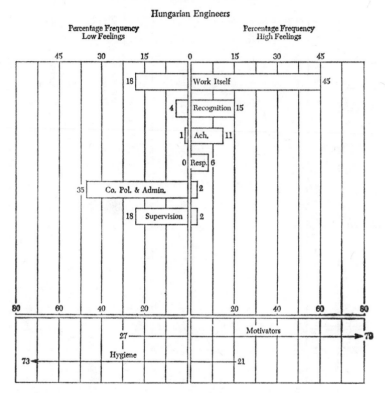

Figure 19

Comparison of Satisfiers and Dissatisfiers

Hungarian Engineers

tables. Table III gives the population of the ten studies just reviewed, their size and the organizations to which they belong. Table IV presents a summary of all the significant findings. Each X in the table represents a correct prediction for a factor, while a dash indicates an incorrect prediction. The blank spaces suggest no significant evidence either way. Reasons for the blank spaces include the failure of an investigator to include the factor in the analysis, the scoring of only the major factors in events (Texas Instruments), the general rarity of a factor occurring (such as *personal life* and *possibility of growth*) and other reasons depending on the nature of the job, as well as an occasional

TABLE III

Populations in 10 Tests of Motivation-Hygiene Theory of Job Attitudes

Investigator	Population	Size of Population	Organization
Herzberg, F. et al.	Engineers and accountants	203	Nine companies representing a cross section of the industry of Pittsburgh, Pa. Included were basic steels, specialty steels, consumer products, light and heavy machinery, industrial instruments, engineering and shipbuilding and a utility
Schwartz, M. et al.	Male supervisors in lower half of management echelons	111	Twenty-one electric and gas companies in the Middle Atlantic and New England states
Walt, D.	Professional women doing analytical work in economics, languages, mathematics and engineering	50	U.S. Government research installation
Clegg, D.	County agriculture administrators	58	Nebraska Cooperative Agriculture Extension Service
Myers, M.	Scientists Engineers Manufacturing supervisors Male technicians Female hourly assemblers	50 55 50 75 52	Texas Instruments Company's installation at Dallas, Texas
Anderson, F.	Registered nurses Skilled engineering service workers Unskilled food and engineering service workers	29 31 35	Veterans Administration hospital

Saleh, S.	Pre-retirees from management	85	Twelve companies in Cleveland, Ohio. Included were three utilities, one bank and eight manufacturers of chemicals, oil, steel and electrical products
Herzberg, F.	Finnish foremen	139	Wide cross section of Finnish industry
Gendel, H.	Housekeeping workers	119	Two Veterans Administration hospitals
Perczel, J.	Engineers	78	Ganz-Mavag Locomotive Works, Budapest, Hungary

TABLE IV

Summary of Factors Which Showed Significant Differences Between Positive and Negative Incidents of Job Feelings Representing 10 Studies of 17 Populations

INVESTIGATOR	HERZBERG ET AL.		CLEGG	WALT	SCHWARTZ	ANDERSON			MYERS					SALEH	HERZBERG	GENDEL	PERCZEL	TOTALS
Population Factor	Accnts.	Eng.	Agri. Ext. Wkrs.	Prof. Women	Util. Supv.	Unsk. Hosp.	Sk. Hosp.	Nurs.	Eng.	Sci.	Mfg. Supr.	Hrly. Tech.	Fem. Assem.	Pre-Retiree	Finn Supr.	Hskp. Wkrs.	Hung. Eng.	
Achievement	X	X	X	X	X	X̲	X̲	X̲	X	X	X	X	X	X	X	X	X	15
Recognition	X	X	X	X	X	X̲	X̲	X̲	—	—	X	X	X		X	X	X	14
Work Itself		X		X										·X	X		X	5
Responsibility	X	X		X	X	X̲						X		X	X	X	X	10
Advancement	X	X		X	X									X		X	X	5
Possibility of Growth				X			X̲											2 51-0
Co. Pol. & Adm.	X	X	X	X	X	X	X̲	X	X	X	X	X		X	X	X	X	16
Supervision-Technical	X	X	X	X	X	X̲	X̲	X	X	X		X		X	X	X	X	13
Interpersonal Relat.-Sup.	X	X			X			X						X	X	X		5
Interpersonal Relat.-Peers		X		—	—	X̲								X	X	X		5-1
Interpersonal Relat.-Sub.			X	—	—									X				2-2
Working Conditions	X	X	X	X	X			X̲							X	X	X	8
Status				X														1
Personal Life	X		X	X														3
Security					X													1
Salary																X		1
TOTALS	9	9	7	8-2	9-1	5	5	5	3	3	3	5	2	9	9	8	6	54-3 105 + 3 = 108

X Correct prediction
— Incorrect prediction
X̲ Correct prediction—sample too small for Statistical Significance test

moderate frequency of a factor for both satisfaction and dissatisfaction. The last reason is discussed in the section on the interpretation of each of the factors.

The chart shows that of the 51 significant differences reported for the six motivator factors, *every one* was in the predicted direction. For the 57 significant hygiene factors, 54 were in the predicted direction. In sum, then, the predictions from the theory were wrong in less than 3 per cent of the cases.

A count of the times each factor was significant sheds further light on the nature of job attitudes. *Company policy and administration* and *supervision* appeared 16 and 13 times, respectively, out of the total of 17 occupations. These two factors seem to be the most notorious causes of job dissatisfaction. Why? The environment is the source of pain for man the animal, and the most obvious and influential environmental factors of the job are the way the company is run and the behavior of the immediate supervisor.

The remaining hygiene factors appearing with moderate frequency as significantly related to job dissatisfaction encompass the other pertinent job environments, *working conditions* and the three categories of *interpersonal relationships*. The factors of *personal life, status* and *security* occur at isolated and specific times. Thus, during a work history and counted over a large population, they would not emerge as major factors when considered in terms of frequency.

The remaining hygiene factor of *salary* is indeed complex. It occurred only once as a significant dissatisfier, while the rest of the time *salary* did not differentiate between job satisfaction and job dissatisfaction. An article entitled "Ominous Trends in Wage and Salary Administration," by Professor David W. Belcher, in the September-October 1964 issue of the American Management Association's Journal *Personnel*, lists one of the ominous trends as "the acceptance of Herzberg's satisfiers-dissatisfiers theory of motivation." Professor Belcher quite correctly goes on to suggest that the theory has been misinterpreted when it has led to the notion that *salary* and *wage administration* have become unimportant. They are important, very important, as a hygiene or dissatisfier factor. Then why does *salary* appear only once as a differentiating factor in the studies using the motivation-hygiene interview procedure? What is the evidence for *salary*'s being so classified?

Salary can be classified as a dissatisfier or hygiene factor on theoretical grounds, since it pertains to the job environment (rewards for doing the job) rather than to the task itself. But, in addition, there is empirical evidence from the motivation-hygiene studies to document the classification. Although *salary* appears as frequently in the high sequences as it does in the low sequences, further analysis of the data not covered in this review shows that when *salary* is associated with a dissatisfaction event, the negative affect on the attitude of the employee is generally of much longer duration than when it appears in a sequence describing job satisfaction. As an affector of job attitudes, *salary* has more potency as a job dissatisfier than as a job satisfier.

The second research evidence for *salary* as a dissatisfier comes from an examination of the interrelationships of the factors within a sequence. When *salary* occurs as a factor in the lows, it revolves around the unfairness of the wage system within the company, and this almost always refers to increases in salaries rather than to the absolute levels. To quote from *The Motivation to Work:*

> It was the system of salary administration that was being described, a system in which wage increases were obtained grudgingly, or given too late, or in which the differentials between newly hired employees and those with years of experience on the job were too small. Occasionally, it concerned an advancement that was not accompanied by a salary increase. In contrast to this, salary was mentioned in the "high" stories as something that went along with a person's achievement on the job. It was a form of recognition; it meant that the individual was progressing in his work. Viewed within the context of the sequences of events, salary as a factor belongs more in the group that defines the job situation and thus is primarily a dissatisfier.

Beyond the theoretical argument and the research evidence for including *salary* in the hygiene category is an obvious cultural reason. All hygiene needs are connected with salary and, because of this, *salary* is the most visible, communicable and advertised factor in all the world of work. *Salary* permeates the thoughts and expressions of people when they view their jobs. In such a circumstance, it is hardly surprising that *salary* often seems to be a satisfier to the individual. If so many hygiene needs can be fulfilled by money, then it is difficult not to conceive of it as a source of happiness. And conversely, so much unhappiness is caused by the lack of money that the alleviation of this unhappiness is easily viewed as a period of happiness. It will be recalled that *salary* emerged as a dissatisfier with statistical significance in the low-level jobs of Negro housekeeping women in the Veterans Administration hospital. Here the deprivation was so great that the above reasons were insufficient to mask the true nature of *salary* as it affects job motivation.

Shifting to the motivator factors, three of the six, *achievement, recognition* and *responsibility,* are the most consistent in producing job satisfaction. These three describe accomplishment, reinforcement for accomplishment and increasing challenge—the basic ingredients of psychological growth. *Advancement* can be visible evidence for psychological growth, but it occurs in only one-third of the studies because of its higher-order nature and because the opportunity for this factor is less frequent than for *achievement, recognition* and *responsibility. Possibility of growth* is a fringe factor, difficult to code, and the objective events containing it are infrequent.

The final factor to consider is *work itself,* essentially but not exclusively coded for expressions of interest in the job task. Two comments on this factor, based on the data of all these studies, appear warranted. First, on the part of many of the employees interviewed there is a lack of interest in the jobs they do. Second, and conversely, the lack of interest in work has produced considerable frequencies of dissatisfaction incidents that reduce the differences between the frequency of work interest in job-satisfaction events. This frequent inversion of *work itself* among many of the employees examined testifies to the importance for humans of occupying themselves with activities that have meaning to them, rather than being passively involved with extrinsic determinants of their productive lives. In Chapter 6, on the motivation-hygiene theory, it was suggested that many persons with strong motivation-seeking qualities become so disappointed with the lack of the motivators that they report themselves as dissatisfied. It was also suggested that this type of report was qualitatively different from the dissatisfaction that is caused by the hygiene factors. *Work itself* is an example of an important motivator that leads to misinterpretation of one's feelings.

There were three statistically significant inversions among the 17 groups studied. All three were in the area of *interpersonal relationships*. The first occurred with the lower-level supervisors working for utility companies, who reported that getting along with their subordinates made them happy more frequently than failure to get along with them made them unhappy. The interpretation of this writer is that their level of management, and particularly the nature of the organizations in which they work, induces a kind of pathology or sickness in their motivational pattern. It is interesting to note that this group was the only one which revealed *security* as a significant factor, a result in line with the psychology of utility companies and with the parallel psychology of their lower managerial employees.

The other two inversions were found with the professional women in government service. They reported happiness from effective *interpersonal relationships* with their subordinates and with their fellow employees. Again, a rational explanation is that a sickness in motivation is brought about by the insecurity of women competing in a traditionally masculine domain.

Similarly, peculiarities of jobs, job situations and types of organizations will interact with individual personalities to produce isolated inversions of the factors that are not revealed in the total statistics. There are, in addition, the inversions stemming from hygiene-seeking employees and from the failure to differentiate positive from negative feelings adequately when a motivator is occasionally given as a source of dissatisfaction.

At the time of this writing, more than a dozen other replications are in progress, testing the theory on still more occupations and organizations. Few studies in industrial psychology have been replicated as often as the motivation-hygiene study, and the evidence appears to be overwhelming that the nature of job attitudes is reflected by the theory first proposed in *The Motivation to Work*.

In the next chapter, those studies that varied the methodology in an attempt to verify the theory by other means will be explored. In addition, the studies concerned with the implications of the theory, particularly for the area of mental health, will be reviewed.

8

Further Verification of the Motivation-Hygiene Theory

ANOTHER OBSERVATION on the motivation-hygiene thesis that is sometimes made is that it may be technique-bound, that is, the results can be confirmed only if identical methods of investigation are used. While this observation does not necessarily discredit the theory, it does raise the possibility that the approach may overdetermine the answers given by the subjects. A related point is that these results may be reflecting a defensive reaction of the subjects to the questions. Those who have suggested this possibility believe that individuals tend to "perceive the causes of satisfaction within the self, and hence describe experiences invoking their own achievements, recognition or advancement in their job. On the other hand, they may tend to attribute dissatisfaction not to personal inadequacies or deficiencies but to factors in the work environment, i.e., obstacles presented by company policies and supervision."

Assuming that there is bias, the probable bias is to obscure the motivation-hygiene theory rather than enhance it. The supposition that people would *prefer* to blame hygiene factors rather than the motivators for their job unhappiness in order to make themselves look good is naive. It does not take too much experience with job-attitude data to find that the opposite is more often true. Employees who wish to make themselves *look good* are much more prone to say that they are unhappy because they do not have responsibility, are not getting ahead, have uninteresting work, see no possibility for growth and do not receive recognition than to say that their supervisor is unfriendly, the administration is poor, the working conditions are bad, their fellow workers are unsociable, etc. The frequency of just such an occurrence is illustrated by the graphs in Chapter 7, on verification of the theory. The charts all reveal that the slippage of factors is overwhelmingly in the direction of blaming the motivators for job dissatisfaction; the motivators arrow is much less unipolar than the hygiene arrow. This is contrary to the surmise registered in the above-quoted criticism. As this review unfolds, the other half of the objection will be shown to be untenable by data provided by the critics themselves. The motivators also were found by these investigators to be the determiners of job satisfaction. The empirical evidence in agreement with the logic of the problem suggests the falsity of the bias conjecture.

To obviate such response bias was one of the prime reasons that the "sequence of events" method was selected in the first place. The "fakeability" of responses and the openness to suggestion that job-attitude scales have shown in the past recommended the motivation-hygiene procedure. While it is not possible to eliminate bias, conscious or unconscious, on the part of the subjects when using verbal methods (written scales or interviews), at least it is much more difficult to conjure up appropriate events in one's life during a patterned interview than it is to respond "appropriately" to items in a questionnaire.

As important, if not more important with preformed scales, is the error so often made of providing predetermined choices of job factors for the employees to choose. Marvin Dunnette in his recent book, *Psychology Applied to Industry*, makes this point in reviewing the original study: "Although these conclusions are important, a more fundamental contribution of the study is that the job factors so identified were allowed to emerge from descriptions of actual job situations rather than being based exclusively on responses to checklists or sets of statements developed ahead of time by the investigator. The job factors derived by Herzberg's classification are more likely, therefore, to reflect things in the job environment leading to employees' approach and avoidance behaviors." The general practice of psychologists of giving lists of factors for employees to rate with respect to their job satisfactions by now should be recognized as the one of the most misleading approaches to the study of work feelings.

However, judgment on this matter is best left to the evidence. In this section, therefore, variations of methodology are explored to examine whether the theory is still maintained outside of the specific procedures that were used in formulating the original findings and interpretations, and continued in the many replications by other researchers. In a subsequent section, investigations that have made successful predictions from the theory will be described.

The first report to be reviewed comes closest to the earlier methods. It is part of a larger study conducted by Dr. Paul Schwartz, of the American Institute for Research, to determine standards of performance for middle management personnel in a large multiunit corporation. Before the performance standards were developed, an investigation was made of the sources of job motivation of the employees in the relevant positions. A modification of the paradigm of the motivation-hygiene methods was required by the practical goals of the whole study, and as a consequence the focus was more on job performance than on job attitudes. Not only were the basic questions different, but the content categories of job factors used in the analysis were also modified to reflect the consultative nature of the investigation. The changes represent significant departures from the methods used in the studies examined in the previous chapter.

In the Schwartz study, a total of 373 third-level supervisors completed a lengthy questionnaire, part of which required them to report two incidents in response to each of the following questions: (1) "Occasionally, something happens to the [title of job] that makes him feel particularly well satisfied with his job, and that stimulates him to contribute even more. Think of the most recent time something like this happened to you." (2) "Occasionally, something interferes with the [title of job] efforts to carry out his job effectively. Think of the most recent time you experienced this kind of frustration."

Both of these questions seem to emphasize the performance of the employee more than his attitudes, and each stresses recent events over the most important events emphasized by the motivation-hygiene procedure. Nevertheless, the questions do deal separately with satisfaction and dissatisfaction, and they reflect actual job experiences or events rather than summary opinions about jobs.

As suggested above, the content analysis of the responses to these questions did not make use of the Herzberg set of 16 job factors, but was based on a separate set of job categories more closely related to the everyday activities of the work under investigation and thereby was presumably more practical for the situation. Also, different factors were used to define the job-satisfaction incidents from those used to define the job-dissatisfaction incidents. Although neither set of factors is the same as the Herzberg set, the factors can easily be divided into those that are *job related*, as opposed to those that are related to the *context of the job*.

A total of 360 reports of positively motivating events was obtained. Of these positive events, approximately 80 per cent fall in the motivator classification. Using the Schwartz categories, 37 per cent of the positive events were listed under the factor of *competence*. Schwartz states that "in the area of *Competence*, the motivating factor in most of the incidents is some tangible indication of productivity or success. The supervisor sees the results, feels good, and is motivated to do more of the same." These 37 per cent of the responses to the question requesting incidents of satisfaction are essentially equivalent to the Herzberg motivator factor of *achievement*.

The second major factor determining satisfaction was a category named *recognition for accomplishment*, which accounted for an additional 43 per cent of the positive events. The subcategories defining this factor are clearly similar to the Herzberg factor of *recognition for achievement*, with the possible exception of *merit increase in pay*. Without the actual events it is difficult to ascertain the correctness of the coding, but, to be conservative, the 6 per cent that this subcategory provided may be allocated to the hygiene side.

The third Schwartz factor that contributed to job satisfaction was *expression of confidence*, defined by the subfactors of *acceptance of one's judgments or ideas* and *responsibility of freedom of action*. The probable corresponding factors in the Herzerg system are *achievement* and *responsibility*. Ten per cent of the factors received this coding.

The remaining factors used by Schwartz appear to have a hygiene orientation, but they received only very minor mention. These include *opportunities to help others* (3 per cent), *extracurricular signs of acceptance* (2 per cent), *praise for company* (1 per cent), *improvement in regulations or procedures* (2 per cent) and *backing or help of superiors* (2 per cent).

There are 340 negative incidents reported in which the vast majority centered on the Herzberg factor of *company policy and administration.* Inasmuch as the question asked was directly related to job interference, the other hygiene factors would not be likely to appear with any frequency. The advantage of the focused question for a specific job analysis finds a disadvantage in limiting the many other areas contributing to job satisfaction and particularly to job dissatisfaction.

The major factors in the Schwartz classification that led to negative job feelings were *ill-advised management decisions, hamstringing procedures or red tape, union activities, poor co-operation from interdependent groups, management apathy toward problems or needs, delay or incomplete instructions and information, interference in management of one's own operations, being by-passed in decisions affecting the job* and *having requests or recommendations turned down.* This list accounted for 76 per cent of the factors coded in the dissatisfaction events.

In summary, *achievement* and *recognition for achievement* were the factors overwhelmingly found in response to the positive question, while *company policy and administration* was the major factor in response to the negative question. Variation in method and response categories did not alter the basic two-factor pattern of job attitudes.

In his paper describing the study of middle managers, Schwartz comments on another investigation by his colleague Clifford Hahn, on the job motivation of officers in the United States Air Force. While Schwartz presented few details, he summarized the Hahn effort by stating, "an analysis of satisfiers and dissatisfiers showed close agreement with the earlier Herzberg findings." Dr. Hahn has kindly made available to this writer some of the original data and analyses, and these are the source for the following description.

Hahn analyzed nearly 1,000 incidents obtained from a sample of about 800 officers from various commands of the United States and Europe. These officers range in rank from second lieutenant to colonel. The incidents were given in response to the following two attitudinal questions: (1) "Think of a recent time during your present or previous assignment when you had what you considered an especially good day on the job, the kind of day you wish most of them were because you felt a sense of personal satisfaction from the day's activities." (2) "Think of a most recent time during your present or previous assignment that you ran into a job situation in which you felt discouraged, frustrated, or just peeved by what occurred to the extent that you questioned the value of an Air Force career for you."

The variation implicit in these questions centers on the short-term nature of the incidents they bring forth by stressing good and bad days. This tends to overemphasize anecdotes on the job rather than sequence of events that have greater impact on the employee over a longer period of time. Nevertheless, two questions are being asked, one for positive feelings and one for negative feelings, rather than the traditional single question for both types of attitudes.

Hahn attempted a number of different types of analyses to classify the responses. The clearest results were obtained when he adopted a classification scheme related to that used by the motivation-hygiene studies. In this instance, the incidents were divided into four categories:

1. Self actions
2. Actions and/or characteristics of superiors or supervisors
3. Actions and/or characteristics of peers, colleagues, subordinates and others
4. Job context

According to this analysis, the major source of job satisfaction (responses to "good" day incidents) was self actions, with 58 per cent of all responses, in contrast to only 1 per cent for the "bad" day incidents. The category of self action includes mostly incidents relating to personal accomplishment and contribution to the job. Perhaps the corresponding categories in the Herzberg system for self actions are the job factors *achievement* and *responsibility.*

The major sources of job dissatisfaction were actions of supervisors (49 per cent) and job context (33 per cent); in contrast, the percentages of these two sources for good day incidents were 2 and 3 respectively.

Actions and characteristics of superiors include ineffective direct supervision of subordinates, ineffective planning or execution of plans, personal integrity and unfair actions. Job factors in the Herzberg system are *supervision, company policy and administration* and *interpersonal relations with supervisors.* It will be recalled that these are the three most potent hygiene factors found in all the other studies.

Under job context Hahn included most of the other hygiene factors, but perhaps also some of the motivators, such as level of responsibility and specific job or duty assignment. It is difficult to determine whether the latter category coincides with the job factor *work interest.* Nevertheless, despite the possibility that some motivators may be categorized in the job-context set, the category is mostly made up of hygiene factors such as family inconvenience, status, equipment and supplies, Air Force procedures, frequency of change in job assignments, characteristics of supervision, etc.

The Hahn study emphasizes, first of all, the importance of the motivators over the hygiene factors in a population where the hygiene factors would appear to be one of the major motivating factors. It is often assumed that the Armed Forces cater to the needs of security, definition and orderliness in jobs. Hahn finds that, on the contrary, the basic need of the officers is to actualize their own potentiality within the tasks of their jobs.

The results also confirm the two-factor theory whereby the sources of dissatisfaction shown in the responses to the "bad" day incidents revolve around the hygiene factors of *supervision, policy and administration, interpersonal relations* and the other assorted hygiene factors, in contrast to the self actions of *achievement* and *responsibility* recorded for the "good" day incidents.

Another successful test of the theory, with considerable variation in method, was accomplished by Dr. Wayne Gibson at Western Reserve University. Gibson analyzed the data from an extensive morale survey conducted by a large Midwestern manufacturing firm. The morale survey was administered to a sample of more than 1,700 employees in four separate plants and ten different departments. Because of variations in the survey questions for different levels of employees, only the data pertaining to the nonsupervisory personnel was applicable to test the motivation-hygiene theory.

The survey consisted of the usual assortment of objective-type morale items with the provision, at the end of the questionnaire, of four free-response questions to which the employees were requested to respond if they wished. Two of these questions, while not the best to elicit the kind of information that suits a motivation-hygiene analysis, were nevertheless promising enough for such an attempt to be made. These were the two questions: (1) "What, if any, are the major irritations, disappointments, or problems related to your job that have not been covered in your answers to this questionnaire?" (2) "What are the things which give you the greatest satisfaction in your job or which make you glad to be in the particular job that you hold?"

Neither of these two questions attempts to elicit job experiences directly; both questions are thus more subject to "opinion" responses at a shallow level of psychological report, but they are nevertheless oriented to a distinction between negative and positive feelings.

Gibson adopted the same 16 job factors for the analysis of the write-in responses that were developed by Herzberg. Because the questions were asked at the end of the survey, and were interpreted by the employees as requesting information not previously covered in the questionnaire, the number of sequences and factors associated with them was far fewer than the number of respondents.

The results for the male employees were in direct accord with the theory. Two motivator factors were found significantly more often in the responses to the question dealing with sources of job satisfaction. Two hygiene factors, on the other hand, were significantly more frequent in the responses to the negative-attitude question. The results are shown in the Table V.

For the females, four of the motivators were significant in the prescribed direction. The smaller sample of women, coupled with

TABLE V   525 Male Nonsupervisors

Factors		Positive Attitude Question	Negative Attitude Question
Motivators	Achievement	22%	1%
	Work Itself	14%	3%
Hygiene	Company Policy and Administration	2%	16%
	Supervision	2%	12%

the fact that they responded very lightly to the negative question, resulted in sparse data on the hygiene factors. Table VI presents these results.

TABLE VI   131 Female Nonsupervisors

Factors		Positive Attitude Question	Negative Attitude Question
Motivators	Work Itself	24%	4%
	Achievement	13%	2%
	Recognition	13%	2%
	Responsibility	11%	3%

There was an interesting addition to this study that takes it beyond a modified replication of the basic findings. It was hypothesized that the two-factor theory would hold when a group of generally satisfied employees was contrasted with a group of generally dissatisfied employees. The basic difference hypothesized was that the satisfied employees would be more satisfied with the motivator factors than the dissatisfied employees, while the opposite would obtain concerning the hygiene factors with dissatisfied employees. To state this hypothesis again for clarity, it was predicted that the sources of satisfaction for both satisfied employees and dissatisfied employees would be the motivator factors, but that the satisfied employees would emphasize them more. In contrast, the hygiene factors would be the source of dissatisfaction for both groups, but more emphasized by the dissatisfied employees.

The means to categorize the employees on their over-all job satisfaction were eight general multiple-choice items dealing with *company pride, community feeling regarding the company, will-ingness to recommend employment to the company, feelings regarding improving conditions, job future, over-all satisfaction with the plant, plans for changing jobs* and *future aspirations with the compnay.*

Those scoring in the highest third of all the nonsupervisory employees were allocated to the satisfied group, while those scoring in the bottom third of the nonsupervisory employees (male and female combined) were allocated to the dissatisfied group. There were 290 males classified as satisfied and 295 males classified as dissatisfied. The corresponding numbers for the nonsupervisory females were 98 and 33, respectively, indicating a higher percentage of females who expressed an over-all satisfaction with their jobs.

When the 290 generally satisfied males were compared with the 295 generally dissatisfied males, the prediction was substanti-ated. The basis of satisfaction for both groups were motivators—the factors of *achievement* and *work itself,* but these two factors were more pronounced for the satisfied employees.

The same three hygiene factors accounted for the dissatisfac-tion in both groups—*company policy and administration, super-vision* and *salary.* Again, as predicted, they were more pro-nounced for the dissatisfied employees. Table VII presents the data.

There were too few responses from the female employees to make a similar statistical comparison.

TABLE VII   Response of Male Nonsupervisors

Factors	POSITIVE ATTITUDE QUESTION		NEGATIVE ATTITUDE QUESTION	
	Satisfied Employees	Dissatisfied Employees	Satisfied Employees	Dissatisfied Employees
Achievement	31%	17%	1%	1%
Work Itself	21%	10%	0%	6%
Company Policy and Administration	5%	0%	6%	24%
Supervision	5%	1%	7%	17%
Salary	6%	6%	8%	18%

Greater modifications in methodology still revealed the two-factor nature of job attitudes. The Gibson investigation also offered confirmation, for the first time, from a successful effort at prediction of the factors as emphasized by contrasting groups of employees. More prediction studies will be presented after the basic replications have been reviewed.

Thirty rehabilitation patients at the Highland View Rehabilitation Hospital in Cleveland were the subjects of an unusual test of the motivation-hygiene theory by Dr. Rainette Fantz of Western Reserve University. The patients were 19 males and 11 females averaging 43 years of age, with a range of from 21 years to 65 years. Six of the 30 subjects could be classified as professionals and the remaining 24 were distributed among skilled, semiskilled and clerical occupations. They were selected to represent three classes of physical disability: (a) ambulatory, (b) nonambulatory, with the use of hands and (c) nonambulatory, without the use of hands.

The study was designed to test the two basic themes of the motivation-hygiene theory. First, do satisfaction and dissatisfaction differences apply as well to experiences other than those related to jobs? In this particular instance, are happy hospital experiences based on the motivator factors and unhappy hospital experiences based on the hygiene factors? Second, does the distinction between motivator seekers and hygiene seekers relate to differences in the success of physical rehabilitation?

The second question will be examined in detail at a further point in the review dealing with experimental examination of the theory. At this time the question is whether two independent sets of factors for satisfaction and dissatisfaction emerge in a totally different and extremely acute life situation. Furthermore, do these factor sets follow the prescribed definition of their make-up, i.e., environment versus individual growth?

The interview procedure for obtaining the data was identical to that of the original study and their direct replications by Myers, Schwartz *et al.*, Walt, Anderson, Gendel, Herzberg, Clegg and Saleh. The content analysis of the interview data also proceeded in a manner similar to that of the basic study but with a major alteration. The factors that were derived from work experiences did not adequately describe the hospital situation of patients.

Such job-related terms as salary, company policy and administration, working conditions, status, advancement, responsibility, work itself, etc., were obviously inappropriate for use in the setting of this investigation. The development of a list of relevant factors for hospital experiences through the long process of rational factor isolation described in *The Motivation to Work* was beyond the scope of a doctoral dissertation; nor was such a tedious task warranted. Instead, a factor system that related well as descriptive of the hospital situation and theoretically as to the motivation-hygiene theory was available in Maslow's set of hierarchal needs. With some slight modifications in Maslow's list, six factor categories were used to classify the "sequence of events" obtained by the interviews. The three lower-level needs of Maslow's scheme were considered to be equivalent in their psychological meaning to the hygiene factors. These needs were:

1. The physiological needs, described by a sequence of events pertaining to the patient's physical condition *not brought about* through his own efforts (e.g., the healing of decubiti).

2. The need for safety, described by a sequence of events that objectively enhanced or detracted from a patient's safety (e.g., movement from bed to wheel chair or the competence of the attending personnel).

3. The need for belongingness, love and other social needs, described by a sequence of events in which relationships with others not directly concerned with medical care were involved (e.g., family visits).

The three higher-need categories adapted from Maslow represented the motivators. These were:

4. The need for autonomy, which included sequences involving self-importance, self-respect, independence and achievements (e.g., success in using a wheel chair).

5. The need for self-understanding, as illustrated by one patient's selection of a sequence involving group psychotherapy in which she had mastered "self-pity."

6. The need for creativity, illustrated by incidents in which the patients gained satisfaction or dissatisfaction from their efforts in occupational therapy.

As in the Myers study at Texas Instruments, each event was coded for only the major factor involved.

From each patient six independent events were obtained: two satisfying and two dissatisfying sequences from his hospital experience and a single satisfying and a single dissatisfying experience from his previous job history. The analysis of the incidents using the above categories included a first level, pertaining to the actual events, and a second level, pertaining to the psychological effect that the events had for the respondent. One other point of methodology is important, especially for the second question of this study. The data was collected at a time in the patients' hospitalization when they were scheduled for rehabilitation service, i.e., when purely medical care had ceased to be their therapeutic regime.

The initial results of this study dramatize the hospital setting. The majority of the events affecting satisfaction are in the area of hygiene. This is not surprising in view of the condition of the patients in terms of their physical disability and of the economic, financial, social and environmental threats to their life. However, as the results unfold, the motivation-hygiene dichotomy breaks through the weighting of the circumstances against it.

The 60 positive and the 60 negative events recorded for the hospital situation are divided as shown in Table VIII.

TABLE VIII   Hospital Events (First Level)

EVENTS	HYGIENE	MOTIVATOR	TOTAL
Good	45	15	60
Bad	59	1	60
Total	104	16	120

Approximately 87 per cent of the events are hygiene events, testifying to the extreme stressful setting. However, of the 16 motivator events given, 15 occurred for a good sequence of events, and the majority of hygiene events is predictably associated with the bad incidents. The difference shown in the table is again highly significant.

At the second level of analysis, the data shows even more striking support for the two-factor theory. Evidently, the many hygiene events in the hospital have their effects because they hold motivator significance for the patients, since one third of the events now are classified in the motivator category. (A perfect relationship would suggest that one half of the events should be hygiene events and one half motivator events.) Both sets of factors shown in the Table IX appear in the predicted direction, with statistical significance.

TABLE IX   Hospital Events (Second Level)

EVENTS	HYGIENE	MOTIVATOR	TOTAL
Good	26	34	60
Bad	53	7	60
Total	79	41	120

Each of the patients, as mentioned above, was requested to review his previous job history for happy and unhappy events in the same manner as in the original study. Only one satisfaction and one dissatisfaction event were elicited, with the results shown in tables X and XI.

TABLE X   Job Events (First Level)

EVENTS	HYGIENE	MOTIVATOR	TOTAL
Good	8	22	30
Bad	19	11	30
Total	27	33	60

TABLE XI   Job Events (Second Level)

EVENTS	HYGIENE	MOTIVATOR	TOTAL
Good	6	24	30
Bad	20	10	30
Total	26	34	60

Once again the results shown in these two tables are statistically significant and, as might be expected, the two-factor theory emerges quite clearly when job experiences are examined.

While no comparison of the factors is possible, since a different factor categorization was required by the investigation, the motivation-hygiene theory finds substantial support when it is expanded to include extra-job feelings.

In *The Motivation to Work* there is a chapter on the effects that the various attitude changes had on the respondents. One of the results described is the relationship of dissatisfaction events with job turnover. Friedlander and Walton carried this idea through in another investigation on the two-factor theory. Their hypothesis stated the "reasons one remains with an organization differ from (and are not merely opposite to) the reasons for which one might leave the organization." The reasons for remaining, they suggest, would be work-process factors (motivators), while the reasons for leaving would be factors in the work context (hygiene factors).

Two questions were asked of 82 scientist-engineers employed by one of the Armed Services' largest research and development laboratories. (1) "What would you say are the most important factors that are operating to keep you here with this organization?" (2) "What are some of the factors that might cause you to leave?" The replies to these questions, shown in Table XII

TABLE XII   Relationship Between Individual Motivations
              and Job Characteristics

TYPE OF MOTIVATIONS	JOB CHARACTERISTICS	
	Work Process	Work Context
Positive motivations-satisfiers (reasons for remaining with organization)	66%	27%
Negative motivations-dissatisfiers (reasons for leaving organization)	20%	80%

reproduced from the Friedlander and Walton article (*Administrative Science Quarterly*, 1964), clearly demonstrated the motivation-hygiene thesis. The motivators are given in a three-to-one ratio over the hygiene factors as reasons for remaining on the job. In contrast, the hygiene factors, as predicted, occur with a four-to-one ratio as reasons for leaving the job.

We turn now to studies that veer toward the more traditional methods of job attitudes. The essential difference between them and the research just presented is that the respondent is provided the list of job attitude factors to rate, rank or select; he responds to the psychologist's choices, not his own. These methods suffer from two major biases, as suggested earlier in this review. First, the meaning of the item as presented to the employee is unclear; and second, there is the unlikely assumption that he is responding to some real job experience rather than to a general opinion. If these biases are kept in mind by the investigator in designing his study and in the interpretation of his results, useful findings are possible.

Friedlander obtained ratings on two identical 73-item questionnaires describing various job factors completed by 1,935 government employees. Two ratings were obtained, the first in terms of the respondents' satisfaction or dissatisfaction with the factor, the second in terms of the degree of importance of the same factors to their morale. When Friedlander correlated these two variables (degree of satisfaction or dissatisfaction with importance of the factor); he obtained no relationship. He then dichotomized the scores into those items marked as satisfied and those chosen as dissatisfied and repeated the correlations. This time he obtained significant relationships. Friedlander concluded that "satisfaction and importance are significantly related if factors are dichotomized into satisfying and dissatisfying experiences. The relationship is positive in the case of satisfying factors and negative for dissatisfying factors."

Two other analyses of this study are significant. "Satisfying and dissatisfying factors are of approximately equal importance. However, factors of extreme satisfaction and dissatisfaction are significantly more important than factors of mild satisfaction or dissatisfaction." The other finding was directly related to the motivation-hygiene theory. "The positive items are concerned almost entirely with work. . . . The most potent satisfiers in order of decreasing importance, were a feeling of achievement in the work I am doing; work requiring the use of my best abilities; and performing challenging assignments on my job." The negative items were composed of pure hygiene factors.

Three verifications of the theory are presented by this Friedlander study: satisfaction and dissatisfaction are not the obverse of each other; the motivators are important to satisfaction and the hygiene factors are important to dissatisfaction, and, finally, extreme satisfactions and dissatisfactions are more important than lesser feelings. This last point warns against attributing too much meaning to items listed in job-attitude questionnaires without being able to separate the wheat from the chaff. The study by Wernimont and Dunnette, to be viewed shortly, is a painful illustration of such naivete.

Halpern constructed graphic rating scales for each of the motivators and each of the hygiene factors and administered them to 93 subjects selected at random from the files of a university educational-vocational counseling center. These subjects had received counseling about ten years before the study. The purpose was to test the theory's claim that even when the employee is equally well satisfied with all aspects of his job, only the motivator factors will be related to job satisfaction. It was found, as claimed, that although the subjects were *equally well satisfied* with both aspects of their jobs, the motivator factors contributed significantly more to over-all satisfaction than did the hygiene factors. Halpern reports that the motivator factors accounted for 43 per cent of the variance in over-all job satisfaction, contrasted with the 16 per cent contributed by the hygiene factors.

A master's thesis by Robert Ewen of the University of Illinois tested a hypothesis similar to that of Halpern with what he interpreted to be no support for the theory. In his investigation, Ewen apparently used a total of seven items selected by factor analysis from a 58-item questionnaire. Two items measured over-all general morale and one item was used to measure each of five job factors. These factors included *manager interest in agents, salary* and *company training* as presumed hygiene factors, and *work itself* and *prestige or recognition* as supposed motivators.

The comment made previously about the meaning of such items to the respondent is pertinent in this case. In addition, two errors are seemingly apparent in Ewen's classification. He lists as a motivator *prestige or recognition*. Prestige is clearly a hygiene factor and thus this item is confounded. One of his motivators is *company training*, which may be interpreted either as belonging to the factor of *company policy and administration* (a hygiene factor) or as *possibility of growth* (a motivator). This leaves three factors with probable relevance to the theory, including *salary*, which is already a confounded factor to begin with, because it so often represents recognition for achievement.

Ewen had life insurance agents rate their degree of satisfaction to each of the items on a four-point scale. Those who checked the most satisfied end were classified as satisfied subjects; those who checked the most dissatisfied end were the dissatisfied subjects; those who checked either of the two middle points of the scale were considered to be neutral or average on the job factor.

He proceeded to predict over-all general morale of the agents (as measured by two items) from their ratings of each of the factors (each assessed by one item). He theorized that if a respondent was neutral on the hygiene factors and high on a motivator, then his general morale should be higher than that of those who were neutral or dissatisfied with the motivator. And he reasoned that since motivators are not dissatisfiers, those neutral on the motivators should be equal on general morale with those dissatisfied with the motivator. To clarify this, we will illustrate with the factor of *work itself* in the following table:

Actual Satisfaction with Work Itself for those Neutral on Hygiene factors	*Predicted General Morale*
High (1 on 4-point scale)	Satisfied (1 on 4-point scale)
Average (2 & 3 on 4-point scale)	Average (2 & 3 on 4-point scale)
Low (4 on 4-point scale)	Average (2 & 3 on 4-point scale)

A similar analysis was done for the hygiene factors with those neutral on the motivators, for example:

Actual Satisfaction with Salary for those Neutral on Motivators	*Predicted General Morale*
High	Average
Average	Average
Low	Dissatisfied

Ewen's findings were that *work itself* acted as predicted by the motivation-hygiene theory. *Prestige or recognition* he found acted as both a satisfier and dissatisfier, a likely occurrence since it was a confounded factor. *Training* acted as a satisfier, but since he called this a hygiene factor he concluded that it did not support the theory. If, however, it is a motivator (*possibility of growth*), then the theory is supported. *Salary* also acted as both a satisfier and dissatisfier, which is expected if it is a confounded factor. The last factor, *manager interest,* was a satisfier, contrary to the theory in Ewen's opinion. Therefore, if Ewen's analysis is taken at face value, his results can be shown to support the theory in four out of five instances.

However, let us look at the logic for a moment, and disregard the outlandish measurement of the complex concepts of general morale by two items and the factors by one item. Ewen had one unconfounded motivator (*work itself*) and two unconfounded hygiene factors (*manager interest* and perhaps *salary*). When he finds that *manager interest* is a satisfier, what is his rationale? If an agent checks "neutral" on the factor of *work itself,* and is satisfied with his *manager's interest* in him, he should not be higher on general morale than those who are neutral on that item. Perhaps, if Ewen had kept all the motivators neutral and not just one, he would have been more sensible in his investigation.

In 1957, my colleagues and I at Psychological Service of Pittsburgh published a book that was an attempt to summarize the research and opinion that had been garnered in the area of job attitudes for the past half-century. The book was a saddening experience, because the major conclusion, I felt, was that we could document almost any position one wished to take with respect to what affected people at work. It was this feeling of hopelessness that led to the formulation of a completely new approach to, and conceptualization of, job attitudes as reported in the follow-up book, *The Motivation to Work.* The survey of the literature, however, did place into focus some of the data that had been continuously reported. By categorizing the various job factors that had been investigated by rating methods, to make sense out of the multitude of such investigations, we were able to call attention to the importance to job satisfaction of the factors we later labeled as motivators. The following four studies testing the motivation-hygiene theory confirm the importance of the motivators.

Fine and Dickman reported a study entitled *Satisfaction and Productivity.* They stated that they were testing two hypotheses. First, "satisfiers will in the main be perceived by workers as having to do with those working conditions which satisfy their need for growth and self-realization within the framework of a career orientation. Dissatisfiers will in the main be perceived as those working conditions relating to social and material needs, comforts, conveniences and security." Second, although the situation described in the first hypothesis may be generally expected for most classifications of workers, it is more likely to occur for those who have a clearly defined career status with "unlimited ceilings than those workers in classifications of jobs that are more limited from a career standpoint." This second hypothesis is contrary to the predictions of the theory and to the evidence from the studies previously cited dealing with lower-level employees. As it turned out, Fine and Dickman's second hypothesis was disproven and the generality of the motivation-hygiene theory was upheld.

A satisfaction questionnaire containing 27 items was developed to measure the relative importance of various working conditions in terms of satisfaction and productivity. Ten items were categorized as satisfiers and the rest as dissatisfiers. The sample included five groups of employees representing high to low occupational levels: senior engineers and physicists, associate engineers and physicists, technicians and technical aides, and secretarial and clerical workers.

When the items were ranked for satisfaction and for immediate influence on productivity, "the top ranking items clearly fulfill the description of Herzberg et al. as factors which lead to positive job attitudes (Achievement, Recognition, Work Skill) . . . because they satisfy the individual's need for self-actualization in his work. The items ranked low are clearly job context factors." These findings held for all their groups. The authors mention that the "satisfiers" not included in the top ten were *supervisory help when needed* and *technical or professional competence of associates,* hardly surprising in view of the fact that they are hygiene factors.

Although Fine and Dickman felt they had confirmed the motivation-hygiene theory, in truth their method allowed only for a partial verification—the importance of the motivators to job satisfaction and productivity. This is all that is possible by such rating methods.

Another test of the theory, by having subjects (part-time students in psychology courses with work experience) rate their satisfactions and dissatisfactions with various job factors, was published by Friedlander. In this instance, the factors were mostly made up of the Herzberg set, with the instructions to rate the items separately as contributing to job satisfaction and as contributing to job dissatisfaction. Friedlander found, as the theory suggests, that there was no correlation between the ratings of the items for satisfaction and dissatisfaction, confirming the concept of two separate continua for positive and negative feelings about jobs. He also found, as Fine and Dickman had, that the motivators were of most importance to job satisfaction, but that in this instance the same applied to job dissatisfaction. Friedlander concluded that only half the theory was upheld. He failed to recognize that his subjects were not responding to actual feelings about a particular real event, but more to a general survey of what is important to general job morale.

A similar finding is reported by Wernimont and Dunnette with a more labyrinthine method. They constructed two elaborate questionnaires, each made up of 50 pairs of items, with each pair consisting of one motivator factor and one hygiene factor. The first questionnaire had the items written in a positive manner and the other questionnaire had them worded in a negative manner. The pairs of items were matched for social desirability, that is, how willing a respondent would be to admit that the item applied to him. These ratings were obtained by asking 30 students in introductory psychology at the University of Minnesota to indicate how much they would like other people to know that they held such an opinion of their job.

The questionnaires were administered to 50 accountants and 88 engineers. The directions preceding the questionnaire contained a typical motivation-hygiene instruction: "Think of a time when you felt very happy (very unhappy) about your job, either your present job, or any other job you have had in the same general line that really made you feel good (bad)—some situation that made you feel you had just about the best (worst) job anyone could have."

After asking the subjects to focus on a specific time in their past work experience, incredibly the investigator worded the response statements in the present tense. For example:

Generally my job isn't too dull or uninteresting for me.

This company is generally fair to me.

The company treats me a little unfairly.

Sometimes my job is a little dull or uninteresting for me.

Three points are apparent. First, having students rate the items for social desirability completely vitiated the importance and meaning of the items. The directions were to "think of a time when you felt very unhappy about your job. . . . In other words, think of some job situation that made you feel you had just about the *worst* job anyone could have." The respondent is then to describe the reasons he felt so unhappy by choosing between items such as:

The company treats me a little unfairly.

Sometimes my job is a little dull or uninteresting for me.

The majority of the items were of this wishy-washy sort.

Second, while the directions are for a specific job event, the items in the questionnaire are in the present tense and become nothing more than a present morale survey.

Third, "since each respondent was obligated to choose one statement from each of the fifty pairs of statements, by placing a check mark in front of that statement, it can be readily seen that some of the items chosen might have little or nothing to do with a given specific situation. In other words, the individual would be forced to choose between two statements, neither of which would be relevant to the situation he had just described." The quotation is from Wernimont's dissertation, omitted in his publication.

The result of this methodology was to reduce Wernimont's questionnaires to simple paired comparison ratings of very poor items. The findings were the same as those obtained with less pretentious approaches: the motivators are more important than the hygiene factors.

In the second part of his study, Wernimont had the subjects double-check those items that were *most important* to their feelings of job satisfaction and job dissatisfaction, and in this instance provided data corroborative of the whole motivation-hygiene theory, as it applies to job attitudes. But he chose to interpret these favorable results when the respondents checked the important factors, on the basis that his subjects were lying and that in his initial ratings of 50 pairs of items the subjects were tricked into revealing the whole truth. A classic illustration of the psychologist's penchant for trying to find out if someone has six toes without taking his shoes off. The actual data is supportive of the theory and only half supportive of the psychologist.

In a recent lead article of the professional journal of the American Psychological Association, the *American Psychologist*, Neville Sanford chided psychologists who act and think this way: "They can define variables, state hypotheses, design experiments, manipulate data statistically, get publishable results—and miss the whole point of the thing."

More solid proof for a theory comes from research studies that have a prediction element to them. Most convincing of all are experimental predictions in which independent variables are varied and the effects on dependent variables successfully forecast. However, experimental designs such as these are hard to come by in attitude research, but approximate designs involving the measurement of predicted relationships between variables by correlations or differences between groups in their response to attitude variables are possible. In this section, prediction and correlational studies testing the theory will be examined. The studies are quite varied in their subject matter, reflecting the wide pertinence that the theory seems to have.

The first three studies were initiated by Dr. Roy Hamlin, my collaborator in writing the papers entitled *A Motivation-Hygiene Theory of Mental Health* and *The Motivation-Hygiene Theory and Psychotherapy*.

The motivation-hygiene theory as applied to people, rather than to factors affecting the attitudes of people on jobs, makes a distinction between those persons who seek happiness from the motivators, motivator seekers, and those who have an inversion of their motivational pattern and attempt to seek positive happiness by an exentuation of the hygiene factors, hygiene seekers.

The first published study to test the mental health part of the theory was conducted on schizophrenic patients by Dr. Hamlin and his student, Robert Nemo, at the Veterans Administration Hospital in Danville, Illinois. The object of this investigation was to see whether schizophrenics who had improved in their illness would show a different motivational pattern than would a comparable group of patients suffering from schizophrenia who were still classified as unimproved. A further extension of the study provided for the analysis of the motivation pattern of a control group made up of students at the University of Illinois.

The motivational pattern was determined by the choice-motivation scale, a forced-choice activity questionnaire in which various occupations and activities were matched and the subjects forced to choose one or the other. Following each choice, the subject was then required to explain the reasons for his choice. It was the reason given that determined the score—the particular activity selected was of no consequence. Each reason was classified as to the determining factor, whether hygiene or motivator.

The results showed that all three groups were distinguished from one another in the predicted direction by the percentage of motivator scores and the percentage of hygiene scores. Table XIII is reproduced from the published article describing this

TABLE XIII   Percent of Total Responses Excluding
Unscorable Schizophrenic Responses

GROUP	MOTIVATOR	HYGIENE
Students	43.5	21.8
Improved	29.0*	28.7*
Unimproved	16.0*	46.9*

* Difference between improved and unimproved: p = .001

study. The percentages add up to less than 100 per cent because of the unclassifiable responses, as well as the inclusion in the study of a few other scoring categories that were being tried out. The average motivator score sharply decreases from that achieved by the normal students to those of improved schizophrenics and further decreases for those schizophrenics who are still classified as unimproved. The reverse is shown for the hygiene scores.

Hamlin and Nemo summarized their paper by declaring, "the results support the general proposition: positive mental health depends to a major degree on developing an orientation towards self-actualization, responsibility, and goal directed effort."

Another of Dr. Hamlin's students, Kenneth Sanvold of the

University of Illinois, followed up the above-described research by further exploring certain deductions from the motivation-hygiene theory. Sanvold introduced his study by stating that the "Herzberg and Hamlin motivator model for psychotherapy postulates that to attain mental health the patient must develop an approach set. The development of this set is seen as resulting from serial satisfying experiences which must include an effortful task associated with the motivator complex consisting of achievement, responsibility, continuity of purpose, recognition, and perception of the work involved as meaningful." Specifically, Sanvold's purpose was to examine the value of the experience of achievement on an effortful task in altering the motivational orientation of schizophrenic patients.

Sanvold also used as subjects improved and unimproved schizophrenics at the Danville Veterans Administration Hospital, with a control group of normal subjects who were volunteers from among the nursing aides. A complex factorial design was used, but in essence he asked each of his subjects to perform tasks that were either inanely simple or rather difficult. In the first instance, the subjects had no difficulty knowing that they had successfully performed the tasks. For the difficult assignments, Sanvold told the subjects that they had done exceedingly well regardless of their performance. In addition to varying the effort required in the tasks, he also varied the purpose given his subjects for doing the tasks. In one instance no reason was given, while the other group was told that performance in the task would be used for selecting patients to participate in more tasks. Sanvold measured the effects of effort and the effects of relating this effort to some purpose, in terms of changes in before-and-after measures of the subjects' scores on the choice-motivator scale previously used by Hamlin and Nemo. Another measure used was changes in the verbal responsivity of the subjects as measured by performance on two cards from the thematic apperception test.

The results showed an improvement in verbal responsivity, as well as in the motivator orientation for all groups who were given effortful tasks that were related to some purpose, thus confirming the basic tenets of the theory. But an interesting additional finding was that relating the task to some purpose was most important for the sicker patients, while it added less to the performance of the improved patients and nothing to the performance of the normal subjects. To quote once again from Sanvold, "at the higher pathological level (unimproved schizophrenia) the presence of a task related context is not only necessary to the development of a motivator set but its absence will lead to a decrease from the original level." In other words, the mentally ill react to the context of the environment of the task in a more exaggerated fashion. The mental patients, to use David Riesman's term, lack inner-directedness.

To check on what appeared to be a difference in the results with regard to motivation between being given effortful tasks to do and being explained the purpose of the tasks that are to be done, another student of Dr. Hamlin conducted an experiment designed to verify and clarify Sanvold's findings. This study, by Anita Graglia, applied a variation of Sanvold's experiment with college students. Basically, she utilized the same paradigm of interposing tasks between before-and-after measures of motivation. The tasks were again divided into easy and difficult, and the purpose of doing the tasks was also divided into no meaning and a stated reason. To test the difference between effort at the task and the relatedness of the task, Miss Graglia measured the effects of these two interposed variables on the willingness of her students to participate in a series of future psychological experiments or their rejection of the experiment. As predicted by the motivation-hygiene theory, the effect of requiring the students to succeed at effortful tasks led to an increase in the preference with which they viewed participation in a list of psychological experiments over their previous ratings of these experiments. In contrast, the effect of relating the task to some purpose was to increase the rejection of these same experiments. The effect of succeeding at an effortful task was to increase the approach motivation of the subjects to participate in future activities, while attempting to improve motivation by giving tasks a contextual relationship reversed the motivation to one of avoidance of future activities.

These two corroborations cast some interesting reflections on an old industrial relations saw: The nature of the job is not important, as long as the employee is given an explanation of what he is doing. Any assembly-line worker tightening bolts a thousand times a day would have predicted these results, despite the belief on the part of some areas of management that the problem is dissipated if the worker is told that he is contributing to a bigger picture. The man with the torque wrench does not feel he is building a Chevrolet; the manager feels it. Quite a difference! Nor does the engineer designing minimal parts feel the way he is supposed to feel because of the concentrated communications programs aimed at giving him a sense of belonging to the big picture.

A further exploration into the nature of motivator and hygiene seeking was made by Haywood and Dobbs of Peabody College in Tennessee. Their study on 100 eleventh- and twelfth-grade boys from the junior and senior classes of the public high schools in Nashville, Tennessee, was an attempt to test the motivation-hygiene theory by determining whether there was any relationship between motivator seekers and hygiene seekers in their orientation to tension-inducing situations. It was hypothesized that the motivator seekers are inclined toward approach behaviors and would, as a part of this inclination, be more ready to favor tension-producing situations. The hygiene seekers, on the other hand, are characterized by a dominance of avoidance goals, and this would be clearly manifested in the desire to avoid tension-inducing situations.

The choice-motivator scale of Hamlin and Nemo, previously described, was again the instrument for classifying the subjects' motivational patterns. Attitude toward tension-inducing situations was measured by the S-R Inventory of Anxiousness, which requires subjects to rate their probable responses to eleven such situations, for example, a new date or climbing a mountain.

The results confirmed the expectations. "There was a significant tendency for subjects who were high in Motivator orientation to be also high in approach motivations, while those who were high in Hygiene orientation are also high in avoidance motivations."

In the section reviewing the basic replications of the motivation-hygiene theory of job attitudes, one of the studies by Dr. Rainette Fantz described how the sources of satisfaction among rehabilitation patients in a hospital related to the motivator factors, while the source of dissatisfaction with their hospital experience related to the hygiene factors. A second part of this study dealt with the prediction of improvement in rehabilitation therapy from a knowledge of the patients' attitudes toward the motivator and hygiene factors.

It was possible to obtain an index of improvement on twenty-one of the original thirty patients interviewed. This index consisted of rating the patients on six scales of independence of functioning. These six functions included independence or dependence in bathing, dressing, going to the toilet, locomotion, continence and feeding. The ratings were made by the occupational therapy department of the hospital twice during the hospital stay. Originally, the patients were rated when they started their occupational and physical therapy, and they were rerated just before discharge from the hospital or three months after they had first been interviewed, whichever occurred first. If the patient became independent in one or more of these functions by the time of the second rating, he was classified as improved. If no further independence was manifested, he was classified as not improved.

The patients were divided into motivation seekers and hygiene seekers on the basis of their descriptions of the events that affected their feelings during their hospital stay and the events from their jobs before their illness. The typical motivation-hygiene interview procedure, which required sequences of events describing happy and unhappy experiences, was used. If half of all six events (four hospital and two work events) that the patients were required to give were based on motivator factors, the individual was classified as a motivator seeker; contrariwise, those subjects for whom four of their six events were classified as hygiene events were labeled hygiene seekers. The results are shown in tables XIV and XV.

Eight of the nine motivator seekers were rated as improved, in contrast to only three of the twelve hygiene seekers who showed

TABLE XIV   Relationship of Motivational Pattern to Improvement in Rehabilitation

	IMPROVED SUBJECTS	NOT IMPROVED	TOTAL
Motivation Seeker	8	1	9
Hygiene Seeker	3	9	12
Total	11	10	21

TABLE XV   Relationship of Work Motivations to
               Improvement in Rehabilitation

	IMPROVED	NOT IMPROVED	TOTAL
Motivator Seeker on the Job	11	6	17
Hygiene Seeker on the Job	0	4	4
Total	11	10	21

improvement—a statistically significant difference. When the subjects were classified with the use of only the job-attitude sequences, a similar relationship to improvement is indicated, although it fails to reach a level of statistical significance because of the small numbers involved.

Table XV suggests that the same motivational ingredients that affect what a person seeks in work will reflect his attitudes in dealing with personal catastrophe.

Turning now to a prediction study within the context of the world of work, we report on the second part of the study by Shoukry Saleh that replicated the basic theory with pre-retirees from managerial positions. This aspect was an attempt to test further the motivation-hygiene theory of mental health by predicting the attitudes of these pre-retirees to their impending retirement.

Saleh's hypothesis was that those with a motivator orientation toward work would be less enthusiastic about retiring than those who were dominated by a hygiene orientation. To accomplish this test he used two measures—one for assessing retirement attitudes and the other for assessing his subjects' motivation direction. The first measure was achieved by the use of a seven-point response scale to the question, "If I were to rate my general feeling about my coming retirement, I would say that I am ——." The choices range from completely satisfied to completely dissatisfied. To measure motivation orientation, Saleh used a paired-comparison test including Herzberg's sixteen job-attitude factors. The scores on this test consisted of the number of times a motivator factor was chosen over a paired hygiene factor. This he called the motivator score. The hygiene score was the reverse, the number of times a hygiene factor was chosen over a paired motivator factor.

The results of the measures showed that most of the subjects were content with their forthcoming retirement, and most of them accordingly scored in the hygiene range. These results are not surprising, for they represent the reality of the subjects' situation, since their retirement is inevitable and their attitudes are in tune with this inevitability. Most of them are in jobs that essentially call for their fulfilling their time obligations rather than performing any more substantial activity; the presence of the motivators in their work is minimal and this is obviously reflected in their low motivator scores.

A younger group of employees tested by Saleh with the motivator scale showed an opposite emphasis, with most of these scores in the motivator range reflecting the opportunity in jobs as the sources of satisfaction.

The direct test of the hypothesis was made by designating those subjects falling in the highest third of the motivator scores on the test as the motivator group, and those in the bottom third of the scores as the hygiene group; both groups were then compared in terms of their attitudes toward retirement.

The results were that the hygiene group was significantly more favorable to the pending retirement than the motivator group, in accordance with the original hypothesis. The scale results were given additional support by an analysis of the comments made by the subjects to an open-end question asking them to describe their feelings about their coming retirement. The percentage of the job-oriented (motivator seekers) who indicated that they would *not* like to retire because they enjoyed their work was about three times as great as that of the context-oriented (hygiene seekers) managers. Saleh concludes, "pre-retirees who stress the environmental factors of the source of job satisfaction have more favorable attitudes towards retirement than those who stress the factors in their jobs would satisfy the needs for self-actualization."

In a follow-up study, Saleh had 350 pre-retirees from the Canadian Government Civil Service rate their present job productivity and also their willingness to retire. He found a substantial relationship between his two measures. Those who were most productive, in addition to not wanting to retire, indicated a strong desire to continue in full-time work after their retirement. The opposite was true for those who felt they were not being very productive.

The motivation-hygiene concepts have been applied to a wide variety of personnel programs in industry, including selection, training, management development, college recruiting, job enlargement, quality control, wage and salary administration, morale surveys; of most importance, the concepts serve as an underlying philosophy for personnel practices. Unfortunately, industrial practice limits the opportunity for gathering research data as well as limiting what can be made public. Three pieces of research with which this writer was involved are of some interest.

In one of these studies, aimed at determining the meatiness of rotated job assignments in a very large corporation, interviews were held with 118 managers after they had completed their rotated job. These interviews were conducted by managers who had had considerable experience with the motivation-hygiene theory, and particularly with the motivation-hygiene interview procedures. The interviewers proceeded to rate the tasks their respondents were given while on rotation in terms of the richness of motivator opportunity. The respondents completed separately a test for satisfaction with the motivators. By dividing the jobs into the three categories of good, fair and poor, reflecting motivator opportunity based on the interviewer's assesssment, it was possible to obtain a near-perfect correlation with the satisfactions expressed with the motivators on the test by the employees.

A second study was concerned with recent college graduates in a special management-development program geared to provide a heavy dose of motivators for the first year of employment. There are two basic rationales for this program: first, to introduce young college graduates to the world of work in a manner that would instill a liking for work itself as opposed to the hygiene rewards and comforts of a job; and second, to find out early in his employment if the recruit can pass muster in terms of job performance and, in that connection, to determine his motivational orientation between motivation seeking and hygiene seeking.

Each trainee was given the choice-motivator scale developed by Hamlin and a simple rating scale made up of five hygiene and five motivator factors. The second scale required him to think of a positive and a negative incident during his training and to indicate which factors were involved.

The directors of each group of trainees, who were also trained in the motivation-hygiene concepts, rated their trainees in terms of their motivation orientation and their job performance. To improve the reliabilities of these ratings, the supervisors of the trainees also rated them on their performance and motivations. Significant correlations were obtained between both measures of motivation orientation and assessments of job performance.

The third industrial study was a carefully controlled experiment designed to verify a basic prediction of the theory. The subjects were highly educated women performing a vital communications function for a large company. For many reasons, their performance, morale and turnover indices were considered to be poor. Matched groups of these employees were chosen to demonstrate the effect of loading the job with the motivators, while at the same time holding all the hygiene factors constant. The inclusion of the motivators was handled in such a way that not even the supervisors of the experimental group suspected that anything really new was happening.

The study was allowed to continue for six months before an assessment of the results was made. This assessment consisted of comparing before and after measures of work performance, job turnover and employee morale; and on all three criteria the experimental group vastly surpassed the control group. These findings were all the more conclusive since an initial investigation has revealed that there *was poor hygiene morale among these employees; and the inclusion of the motivators had increased the difficulty of the work with no increase in hygiene rewards.* Figure 20 shows the results for the improvement in morale scores and Figure 21 shows the improvement in performance.

The results of the many studies reviewed indicate a striking consistency. The original findings have been extended to a series of diverse populations working in many different types of organizations and by diverse data collection and analytic methods.

Before I close this review, I should like to give a description of the first empirical study of job attitudes conducted in the Soviet Union.

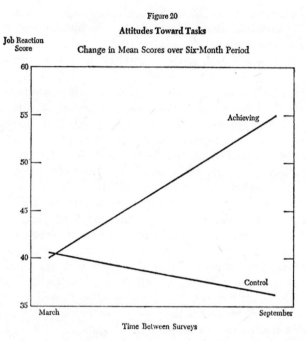

Figure 20

Attitudes Toward Tasks

Job Reaction Score

Change in Mean Scores over Six-Month Period

Time Between Surveys

Early in 1964, I received a communication from Professor Vladimir Yadov, head of the Sociological Research Laboratory at the University of Leningrad, requesting copies of my books *Job Attitudes* and *The Motivation to Work,* as well as other publications to assist him in the preparation of a study of worker attitudes in Leningrad industry. As a follow-up to the initial request, I was invited to visit with Professor Yadov's staff and other members of the Institute of Philosophy at Leningrad, to discuss their research and to lecture on my own theories of job attitudes. The following is a description of this landmark study in the U.S.S.R., based on my personal talks with the Soviet investigators A. G. Zdravomyslov and V. A. Yadov, and on a subsequent translation of an article the Russian authors prepared for publication in the Soviet journal *Questions of Philosophy.*

The stated primary purpose of this pioneer investigation was to "provide information to be used in the proper education of the Soviet youth to the Soviet attitude to labor." It appears that in the Soviet Union there is concern with the motivation of the

Figure 21

Performance Index

Performance
Index   A Three-Month Cumulative Average

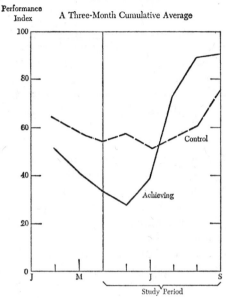

younger generation, just as there is in most of the other nations of the world. In addition, although this was not directly revealed, the Soviet investigators were prompted to carry out this survey for many of the same reasons that we conduct such surveys in the United States. These problems include the traditional ones of absenteeism, labor turnover, low morale, grievances, alcoholism and moonlighting.

The study was conducted on a sample of 2,665 workers under the age of 30, employed in a variety of heavy and light industries located in and around Leningrad. The method included an attitude questionnaire, which was administered by face-to-face interview with the workers, and a work-performance rating obtained from employees' supervisors.

The attitude questionnaire tried to determine the over-all satisfactions the workers had in regard to their job, their trade and the social value of the work they were doing. In addition, the workers ranked various job factors as to how well they are presently satisfied and dissatisfied with them. The level of satisfaction expressed by each of the workers was then compared with his performance on the job. In each instance it was found that those who were more satisfied with their job, with their trade and with the social value of the work they were doing were rated as superior in performance. However, there is an interesting ranking among these three relationships. The highest relationship between satisfaction and performance was with satisfaction with the nature of the work that the employee was doing; the next highest relationship was with his job, and the lowest relationship was with the social value of the work itself.

The Soviet investigators conclude that these results indicate that the most effective and the most important attitudinal factor for effective job performance is satisfaction *with the kind of work*. They go on to expand on the significance of satisfaction with the kind of work that a man does by pointing out that "to view this as only an additional potential for increasing productivity of the worker would imply an extreme utilitarianism. The feelings of satisfaction with work, the cheerful state of spirit, optimism—this is the general emotional background which provides a favorable condition for successful educational efforts in general." And, on the contrary, they continue, "a depressed feeling generated by the concrete conditions of the kind of work done, will also impinge on the attitudes towards other sides of life, which are not directly connected with employment. Thus, a negative emotional background is created. The pessimism caused by these factors becomes a susceptible ground for assimilation of backward and unhealthy views, habits, and biases." Shades of industrial mental health!

Because of the finding that the character and the content of the work have the most influential role in the production of job attitudes, the Soviet investigators proceeded to subcategorize their sample into six groups comprising different levels of job skill. These six groups were physical laborers, manual skilled laborers, machine operators, assembly-line workers, automated machine workers and repairmen of automated machinery.

The results showed that, in addition to having the poorest performance on the job, those in the physical labor group indicated the least satisfaction with the work, with their particular trade and with the social value of their job. The highest satisfaction and best performance were recorded by those workers with the highest skills—those in charge of the maintenance of automatic machinery, followed by those who were in charge of automatic machinery without the repair function. While it is true that the most satisfied group also received the highest pay, the laboring group with the lowest satisfaction was the second highest paid of the six subsamples studied.

Further clarification of these results was obtained by an analysis of the specific factors on the job with which the workers were most satisfied and the factors with which they were least satisfied.

The sample was divided into two groups—workers with very favorable attitudes to their jobs and workers with very unfavorable attitudes to their jobs. Each job factor was then examined for its role in differentiating between these two groups.

The content of the work was found to be the factor that most separated the satisfied workers from the dissatisfied ones. The next factor that most discriminated between these two groups was the wages paid, followed in order by the possibility of improving skills, the variety of the work, the organization of the work, the attentiveness of the management's attitude, the physical strain of the work, the importance of the product being produced and the smooth flow of the work. The least discriminating factor of all was the relationship with fellow workers. This last factor was least discriminating primarily because both satisfied and dissatisfied workers in Russian industry rated themselves as highly content and therefore no discrimination was possible. These are the major results reported by the Russian social scientists.

The following are some of the conclusions they draw from these results:

> The basic factor which imparts the greatest influence on the attitude to work is the content and character of the work itself. The possibility for improvement of skills which will depend on the character of the work and how it is organized is of special importance for the young worker. It would not be an exaggeration to say that the most important and possibly decisive factor that affects man's morale state is his productive activity, his successes and failure in his work.

The Soviet worker realizes more and more deeply that the prospect of his development lies not in the sphere of consumption but in the plane of production. In the socialist society the productive activity becomes the basic content of the interests of the workers. Thus the initiative of a worker expressed by active participation in rationalizing the production process in the industrial undertaking and so forth, is evidently, one of the most substantial peculiarities of the new attitude of labor. The initiative is a method of the assertion of the worker's individuality which is a characteristic of socialism. The initiative is connected with the development of the feeling of proprietorship in the socialist undertaking. A feeling that is unthinkable in the conditions of a capitalistic society.

It is interesting to note that the Soviet sociologists are preaching the Protestant ethic to us! The denigration of the attitudes of the American workers is based on their citing a few studies in the American literature that stress security as the overriding need of the American worker. If the Soviet investigators were more familiar with the American literature, they would find that, contrary to their interpretations, the content of the work that the employee is required to do would be similarly at the top of the list of an American survey—that the Soviet findings would be right in line with the majority of the studies that have assessed the attitudes of the American work force.

It is hoped that when further communication and exchange of data with the Soviet investigators become possible, cross-cultural comparisons will serve to limit the ideological intrusions into the research within the area of behavioral and social science.

One further quotation from the Russians with respect to their study has significance for all countries that are becoming caught up in the dilemma of automation:

After the victory of a socialist revolution the decisive factor in transforming work into the primary life need consists of the elimination of hard physical labor by means of complex mechanism and automation of the industry. Then the production process, by the very character and content, will provide the possibility for the multifaceted development

of the individual. In the case of the unskilled manual la-
borer, the widening of his mental horizon and the increase
of his education does not improve, but rather, worsens his
attitude to work and it impels him to quit his job. In this
case the appeal to the social value of labor hardly helps,
since other work is more useful to society due to its greater
productivity. It is not by accident that the manual labor
group was found in our research to be the least stable.

Perhaps a more realistic psychological view of their conclusion
would be a restatement of the next-to-last sentence in this para-
graph, as follows: In this case, the appeal to the social value
of labor hardly helps, since other work is *more meaningful to the
individual*—not, as the Soviet sociologists suggest, since it is more
meaningful to society.

9

What Do We Do?

THE INVESTIGATION of the two dimensions of man suggested in the previous chapters is inhibited by a seeming paradox in the science of human behavior, for when we study man in detail, we discover only his avoidance nature. It appears that the traditional analysis of human behavior may very well hinder man from seeing his uniquely human characteristics. It is only when we study man as a totality, and see him in terms of his true perspective and proportions, that the Abraham concept comes through. Let me summarize the basic nature of man as presented earlier.

First, I suggested that man is Adam, that he is an animal and that his overriding goal as an animal is to avoid the pain inevitable in relating to the environment. This avoidance nature is determined by man's biological inheritance. As we study man in detail, more and more of the basic mechanisms that determine his reactions to environmental stimuli are found, and the means by which man has broadened his avoidance goals so extensively are delineated. In fact, psychology has made its greatest contribution in making lawful the content of man the animal.

When we look at man in his totality, however, we find that in addition to his avoidance nature there exists a human being—a human being who seems to be impelled to determine, to discover, to achieve, to actualize, to progress and to add to his existence.

These needs summarize the Abraham concept of man. We cannot hope to gain a clue to Abraham by microscopic analysis, nor can we hope to gain an understanding of Adam by macroscopic procedures.

The most essential understanding that emanates from these essays is not only the fact that man exists as a duality but also that the two aspects of man are essentially independent; furthermore, each aspect has a system of needs that operate in opposing directions. Meeting the needs of one facet of man has little effect on the needs of the other facet. When we think of man, we must ask two questions. First, how happy is he? Then a distinctly separate question: How unhappy is he? If a starving artist is questioned about his job satisfaction, he might reply that he loves what he is doing but is much dissatisfied with his hygiene. Typically, measurement psychologists would have given him a 50-per-cent morale score and thereby missed the whole point. He answered correctly, but our traditional unitary approach has destroyed the meaning of his answer.

This theory of motivation opens the door wide for reinterpretation of industrial relations phenomena. To repeat, job attitudes must be viewed twice: What does the employee seek? What makes him happy? Then a separate question arises that is not deducible from the first: What does he wish to avoid? What makes him unhappy? Industrial relations that stress sanitation as their *modus operandi* can serve only to prevent dissatisfactions and the resultant personnel problems. Of course, attention to hygiene needs is important, for without it any organization will reap the consequences of unhappy personnel. The error lies in assuming that prevention will unleash positive feelings and the returns of increased creativity, productivity, lowered absenteeism and turnover, and all the other indices of manpower efficiency.

One additional deduction from the theory, which is supported by empirical findings, should be noted. The effect of improved hygiene lasts for only a short time. In fact, man's avoidance needs are recurrent and of an infinite variety; therefore, we will find that demands for improved salary, working conditions, interpersonal relations, etc., will continue to occupy the personnel administrator without any hope of his escaping the question,

What have you done for me lately? Hygiene acts like heroin—it takes more and more to produce less and less effect.

Industry, as the dominating institution in our society, must recognize that if it is to use human beings effectively, it must treat them in terms of their complete nature rather than in terms of those characteristics that appear to be suitable to their organization. Industry cannot progress by continuing to perpetuate a half-conceptual view of man. As already suggested, its present personnel programs, which in effect serve to minimize the natural symptoms of an amputated individual, can lead only to temporary, opiate relief and further the basic psychic pathology. Work stoppages and strikes, which do not seem to be rational in terms of the "enlightened" personnel management of today, are an obvious illustration. Equally obvious to many in industry are the social legislation and government interference that industry often feels go beyond the amelioration of real needs. Not only problems dealing with the unions and social legislation, but other, similar problems as well, are found in the day-to-day operations of business. I refer to the slow crippling of companies by such things as resistance to specific changes, unexpected failures, damaging interpersonal clashes, absenteeism, turnover, psychosomatic illness and similar failures, which can accumulate over a period of time. And, of course, there are the large failures that result in crisis situations.

But, in addition to the compounding of the problems of industry that result from an inadequate definition of employee needs, there is the additional damage of sloughing off too much of man's creativity. Initially, this reduction in creativity is looked upon as the controlled use of man's Abraham nature, because management fears that the need to be creative would run roughshod over the rational administration of the company. Typically, the creative man has been restricted and channeled to serve narrow and specific purposes of the company. This restriction and channeling may then lead to bureaucratic goals that are not designed to provide for the most efficient use of creativity but rather are actuated by fear of it. No institution can long remain dominant or successful if it *overdetermines* the control of man's creativity and his achievement nature. I can quote, perhaps, no better authority than a man who certainly should have learned this lesson well. He is András Hegedüs, the former Prime Minister of Hungary during the Stalin era. In a recent study entitled *Optimization and Humanization on the Modernization of Management Systems,* Hegedüs concludes that "if optimization comes into the foreground, humanistic motives will be pushed into the background and, as a result, bureaucracy will become preponderant and finally the interests of optimization itself will be damaged."

What recommendations can be made to industry in order to carry out the ideas propounded in this book? I am tempted to reply that if I had the answers, I would program them and make a living in a much easier way than by writing books. And in truth, this *is* the task of those who are responsible for the management of organizations, and not the task of psychological critics. In fact, it is this area of management that has been most bankrupt in creativity.

There is one organizational change I feel is essential if we are to structure human institutions to meet man's needs and to reflect the dual structure of his nature as well. This reorganization would separate present-day industrial relations into two formal divisions. One division would be concerned with the hygiene-need system of the employee and the other section would be concerned with his motivator needs. The former, dealing with hygiene, is already well established in companies, and this area of industrial relations will continue to be as important in the future as it has been in the past. The challenge here is a frustrating one. The hygiene needs of the employees for money, fringe benefits, human relations, etc., will inevitably recur and escalate. This is the nature of Adam, and those in charge of this type of program are faced with the continuing necessity of assessing dissatisfaction within their companies. There will be a continuing need for ingenuity, both to raise the level of the hygiene returns and to make sure that each increase maintains a balance of fairness within the minds of the employees. It must also be realized that there are no permanent solutions for sanitary engineers. It should be recalled that the Adam nature of man has these characteristics: an infinite capacity for continuous acquisition of new dissatisfactions, as well as the recurrence of past dissatisfactions. Man's endless learning capacity, his conditioning to the feeling that being "less than" is unpleasant, and the cyclical nature of his primary drives and all the learned drives that are derived from them, insure these characteristics. This book suggests little in the way of advance in procedures for traditional industrial relations, primarily because of this endless nature of hygiene requirements. The theory's contribution is to recognize what can be gained from these procedures.

The second division of industrial relations, then, would be concerned with the motivator needs and have as its sphere the psychological growth of the personnel in the organization. This division would be given the tasks of discovering the problems that interfere with growth and seeking solutions that would encompass technical and psychological procedures. In terms of specific functions, the motivator division would have three basic tasks: the education of employees for motivator orientation, that which is generally referred to as job enlargement and remedial or therapeutic actions.

Let us examine the first task—the re-education of workers and management in terms of a motivator orientation. It was suggested previously that one of the implications of Frederick Taylor's work on scientific management was that the workers acted as they did because of the way they were managed. I suggest also that the workers believe the way they do because their beliefs are the beliefs of management. Industrial relations managers for the past half-century have so successfully promulgated hygiene needs as the reason why people work and are loyal to organizations that employees have come to agree with management, even employees who belong to the most militant unions.

Historically, it has been the preference of human organizations to hold the view and to teach that man is almost completely in his Adam state. Two reasons for this can be suggested. First, it appears easier for institutions that operate with short-range goals, despite verbiage to the contrary, to define man in terms of his avoidance needs. To the institution it seems easier to motivate through fear of hygiene deprivation than to motivate in terms of achievement and actualizing goals. Second, since man's Abraham characteristic reflects his codetermining need, no organization relishes the thought of the individual's determinisms in competition with its own basic goals. Rather than have man compete as a determiner, the organization much prefers that these human characteristics of man be markedly restricted and utilized only in the most controlled, officially sanctioned manner. The Adam concept has been taught and has prevailed in institutions because it leads to the simpler procedure of motivating through fear and because it obviates the necessity of competing with man's actualizing goals.

The implementation is restricted also because the Abraham nature of man is so convenient a concept in terms of the use of traditional slogans. By this I mean that the concepts of initiative, incentive, individuality and achievement are usurped for hygiene purposes. They are the lip service paid by organizations (right-wing groups as well as those on the left) that believe that the best use of the values of Abraham are to sell hygiene needs. To the radical right, the argument for individuality, freedom and private initiative is for the purposes of denying economic and other hygiene gains to aspiring people and of protecting their own gains. It seems they are less concerned about the ethics and driving ethos of our historical traditions than about the fact that the underprivileged seem to be getting some hygiene without sufficient sacrifice. Negroes on relief, I might remind my radical right-wing friends, are providing a service in return for their welfare payments. They are serving a powerful hygiene need, that of satisfying the white man's ego by being second-class citizens. In the chapter on psychological growth, the highest level of growth described is the ability to find a sense of individuality without doing so at the expense of others.

Many corporations whose basic actions are quite socialistic in terms of providing cradle-to-grave benefits are precisely those corporations that, in their communication systems, propagandize the value of the American heritage in terms of its Abraham nature. But, realistically and fundamentally, they do this in the hope of hygiene rewards.

Such propaganda never was concerned with an Abraham need. The felony has in a sense been compounded, because not only does the propaganda fail to satisfy an Abraham need but it also seduces the individual into an incorrect vision of his Abraham nature, and thus further blocks the recognition of his human attributes by both the individual and the organization.

Probably one of the most destructive misinterpretations of the American way of life has been to belittle, attenuate and degrade the concept of the worker's initiative and achievement as pursued for economic profit. Man does work for profit in order to avoid pain; but in a positive sense, he works to enjoy the excitement and meaning that achievement provides for his own psychological growth and thereby his happiness. The limitation of goals by those in industry to that of profit is contradicting and reducing our nation's great heritage. It suggests that there is no nobler purpose in the American experiment than the satisfaction of the avoidance needs of animals.

Even today, we find people who suggest that the profit motive is the incentive to Abraham. It is rather the incentive to Adam, and I hasten to add that this is not inherently wrong or inherently bad, for man's Adam nature is just as real as his Abraham nature. I mean only to reiterate that the confusion of man's Adam and Abraham characteristics leads to the diminution of Abraham. Man is entitled to all the hygiene rewards that are possible in this world. This is the normal and desired result. The point is that when man forgets the purposes of the material rewards that cater to his Adam goals, he does disrespect and damage to his Abraham character. Those individuals who are successful in minimizing their pain by economic success should have much more opportunity to actualize their Abraham motives. Too often, it is precisely the people in the most advantageous economic situation who proclaim that Abraham emerges from Adam.

Adam is not good or bad—he exists. Abraham is not good or bad—he also exists. I must say, over and over again, that I am *not* in any way downgrading Adam; I am merely suggesting that the worshipping of Adam can lead to the loss of Abraham, and this is the unhealthy aspect.

There is nothing wrong with providing the maximum of hygienic benefits to the employee. The benefits should be as great as the society can afford, despite the cries of anguish that have always accompanied the amelioration of work hygiene. What is in error is the summation of human needs in totally hygienic terms. The results of this one-sided view of man's nature have led to untold consequences of much greater import than the direct monetary costs of these programs to our organizations. The more pertinent effect has been on the psychological premises of industrial relations, and its effect, in turn, on the self-concepts of the employees.

Pride in work, in successful accomplishment, in maximizing one's talent, is becoming gauche or, tragically, it is becoming a victim of progress. We cry for the nurturing of human talent and find that we have no place for most of it; human talent on the job has become as much a surplus commodity as wheat. And where are our personnel managers? Their problem is hygiene, not the creative function of maximizing human resources.

The Protestant ethic is being replaced by an avoidance ethic in our world of work, and those in charge of personnel utilization have almost totally directed their efforts to maintenance procedures. This is seen at the very outset of employment, in the practice of college recruitment on the campus: each company sets up its own enticing tent, and selection is transformed into public relations, the luring of candidates, and what has become in fact the incredible situation in which the candidate interviews the interviewer.

Job-attitude data suggests that after the glow of the first year on the job, job satisfaction plummets to its lowest level in the work life of individuals. From a lifetime of diverse learning, successive accomplishment through the various academic stages and periodic reinforcement of efforts, the entrant to our modern companies finds a situation in which work does not provide an expanding psychological existence but, in fact, the opposite occurs, and successive amputations of his self-conceptions, aspirations, learning and talent are the consequences of earning a living. As the needs and values of our industrial enterprises have become the template for so many aspects of our lives, the universities are preparing many young people by performing the amputations early. The university graduates enter already primed for work only as a means of hygienic improvement, or, for those who are still capable of enjoying the exercise of their human talents, as a means of affording satisfaction off the job. If the number of management-development programs designed to re-educate managers is a valid sign, the educational system has done its job only too well.

There is much criticism today of compulsory retirement policies, as the personal consequences of organizational definitions of human obsolescence emerge. Before retirement itself, moreover, there are from thirty to forty years of partial retirement and partial commitment to work for the too many who have not "succeeded" in terms of organizational advancement. From the first orientation to the farewell party, the history of work careers is a history of human waste. What a paradox we face! There is a shortage of talent in the country at a time when our problems are defined in planetary dimensions, and to meet these circumstances we have evolved a system and a philosophy to use and motivate our talent that serve to decrease further this precious resource.

Another teaching objective of the division of motivation would be to alter the basis of loyalty to the company from that embedded, in a sense, in hygiene to that of a more mature loyalty based on self-fulfillment. The quotation from professors Yadov and Zdravomyslov is most pertinent here. They felt that the Soviet workers who found little challenge in their jobs could not be motivated by appeals to their loyalty to the social value of their work. If the Russians can admit to such a conclusion, perhaps the leaders of our free-enterprise organizations can glimpse this truth once they honestly view their industrial relations.

To undo the brainwashing of employees, by recognizing and reorienting the content of communications to employees, would be the first function of the division of motivation. This reorientation must give both sides of man in their proper relationship. Further deceit by using only the words about Abraham will enhance the sickness. Many of the companies for which I have consulted have found effective means of accomplishing this reorientation in work attitude, but I hasten to add that the reteaching must be accompanied by substantive deeds to bring the jobs into line with the new philosophy.

This leads us to the second task of the division of motivation—job enlargement. Today there is a dim awareness that industrial engineering has perhaps gone too far in the process of work rationalization and work efficiency. It appears to me that this concern arises from the law of diminishing returns, which seems to have been reached not only in terms of reducing errors but also from a concern with the morale problems that are becoming more expensive, in many instances, than the costs saved by improved work methods. Unhappily, little of the new attention to job enlargement is prompted by a genuine concern for the fulfillment of employees.

What rules should govern attempts at job enlargement? Certainly we have learned from the bad experience with the rotation of assignments of new recruits into management that the mere exposure to a variety of assignments, with little opportunity for mastering any one, fails as a motivating system. The most promising program I am familiar with that broke this demoralizing practice (in the motivator sense) for new college employees is the Initial Management Development Program of the American Telephone and Telegraph Company.

A discredited direction to job enlargement has been the addition of meaningless snippets of various activities to a job. This approach serves more to aggravate the condition than to ameliorate it. Two or three meaningless activities do not add up to a meaningful one.

What are the criteria for a meaningful job that the motivation-hygiene theory would recommend? To answer this question we must recall what the motivators are, as well as the principles of psychological growth described in Chapter 5.

The following chart is an attempt to relate motivators to levels of psychological growth, to dictate the ingredients that man requires on his job if he is continually to find satisfaction in doing it:

Motivator	Growth Principle
Achievement and recognition for achievement	Opportunity to increase knowledge
Responsibility	Opportunity to increase understanding
Possibility of growth	Opportunity for creativity
Advancement	Opportunity to experience ambiguity in decision making
Interest	Opportunity to individuate and seek real growth

First, the job must allow for some achievement opportunities, and these achievements must result in the employee's knowing more about his occupation or job than he did previously. The recognition for achievement is the reinforcement that is necessary at the early stages of all learning. Eventually, it is hoped, the employee will develop his own generator and will thus rely less on outside recognition of his growth and more on his own evaluation.

Second, increased responsibility suggests a more complex task. Increasing the complexity of the job can provide the opportunity for understanding the relationships among the various components of the assignment and thereby provide for the next level of psychological growth.

Third, the task must contain an open end in its description, to allow for possible growth. If the job allows for possible growth, it may then provide the opportunity for the employee to be creative and satisfy the third level of psychological growth.

Fourth, advancement in the formal sense, or even without change in rank, requires in either case that a higher order of task be presented to the employee. This higher-order task gives the opportunity to be successful in ambiguity and thus leads to a still higher level of psychological growth.

Finally, if the employee finds that the actual task he has to do is of direct interest to him, then his job can provide a sense of personal worth and individuality. Furthermore, if the job has intrinsic attractive powers, the employee is less likely to be concerned with other people's hygiene and less tempted to seek substitute growth from his own hygiene needs. In this latter instance, he is enabled to experience the highest level of psychological growth.

Obviously, no job can provide all these ingredients at one time. Nor, perhaps, can all jobs provide all these ingredients at different times. However, some of these components of psychologically rewarding jobs must be present.

The staff of the motivator division would need to plan and review the growth potential of jobs along the lines suggested. Such an analysis of job content would be constantly required to insure that the jobs do not fit like shoes for a five-year-old when the child is eight. This requires a built-in fluidity to job structures.

Inasmuch as most bureaucracies delight in static organizations while the world can be validly viewed only in terms of process, we find an obstacle in thinking of jobs as being subject to constant change while the organization desires to think of a harmonious set of unchanging positions. Some psychologists have contributed to the bureaucratic concept of jobs by emphasizing the need for an employee's knowing exactly what his job is and what is expected of him. Harry Levinson, director of the Industrial Mental Health Program of the Menninger Institute, considers this need for the reduction of the ambiguity of jobs as one of the employee's most essential psychological requirements. This need for a structured job is valid in order to attune oneself to a bureaucracy, but it is not necessarily valid as a basic need and certainly not for those individuals who are oriented by a growth motivation. However, as pointed out again and again in this thesis, organizations and people are subject to laws, just as the physical environment is. We have long since given up alchemy in dealing with the physical environment. The great advances in the physical domain of man's life have been made when process is substituted as the basic pattern of reality rather than an unalterable structure.

The third function of the division of motivation would be concerned with three major areas of remedial work, which quickly suggest themselves: first, technological obsolescence; second, poor performance among employees, and third, administrative failure. A comment on each of these three is in order.

Employees of all levels of training and education can become obsolescent all too quickly today, as the technology that finds practical use in industry advances and changes at an increasingly rapid rate. Not only are the unused talents of so many people at work wasted, but even the talents that find expression in jobs today may tomorrow join the abilities that were never used. These conditions, which are now felt as emerging problems, will be tomorrow's nightmare in personnel management. The envisioned division of work motivation can very well begin its activities by tackling this problem as a prototype for the larger motivator problems in industry.

There is an older personnel problem that may very well find solutions through plans for outwitting the obsolescence of skills. I refer to those people who have not succeeded or who have not performed up to expectations. At the lower and middle management levels, hygiene has reached a point in most major corporations of providing job tenure similar to seniority rights among the rank and file. The tragic loss of manpower to industry, as well as the personal tragedy of being shelved, is begging for some creative personnel action. The practice of letting people die on jobs, particularly because of failure, provides the devil with an extra dividend. The shelving of managers causes apprehension among the other managerial employees, who quickly inhibit their own creative impulses in order to insure their security. A motivator organization in a corporation should be geared to finding solutions to aid the "failure" and the nonproducer. As handled by line management, these casualties are left at the roadside while others get on with the business. Many psychologists have found, contrary to earlier opinion, that some anxiety associated with work is a healthful force in leading to achievement. This view can easily be misinterpreted. If what is meant is the anxiety concerning punishment for failure, then the result will be the inhibiting effect suggested above. However, if the anxiety stems from the desire to achieve in a task with sufficient ambiguity, then indeed this anxiety reflects part of the growth process and is accordingly a very healthy sign. The first type of fear leads to the intolerance of ambiguity and the consequent performance on the job by playing it safe—an overdeterminism that acts detrimentally both to the individual and to the company. The second type of fear is part of the excitement of discovery.

Finally, the division would be charged with a periodic review of company policy practices, assumptions, rules and regulations in order to assess their continuing value and to engage in a spring housecleaning for those found wanting. Perhaps this review would work hardship on those who find their hygiene in implementing rules, but the motivator staff would be doing some good even for them. There is little growth in being a bureaucrat, and the employee in such a situation would receive the therapeutic benefits of doing something more basically rewarding.

What would be the results of formally dividing industrial relations into these two divisions, and particularly of following through with the tasks assigned to the motivator division? It is predicted, and much scattered evidence seems to be available today in support of the view, that there would be a sharp and dramatic increase in the productivity at the creative level. It cannot help releasing much of the lingering surplus potentiality in companies. We diagram the results as follows:

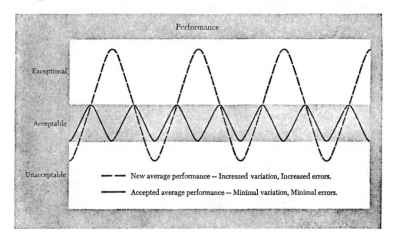

Performance

Exceptional

Acceptable

Unacceptable

— — — New average performance — Increased variation, Increased errors.

———— Accepted average performance — Minimal variation, Minimal errors.

We see that, in addition to the increase in creative productivity, an increase in the errors at the operational level would follow. And, as the diagram suggests, the increase in the creative level would more than offset the total errors engendered by the freedom given the individual. Though there can be agreement on the fact that the increase in creativity would in the long run more than offset the cost of the increase in operational errors depicted in the diagram, there are two things wrong with this suggestion. One is that we cannot go back to inefficient methods in order to provide for more creative use of people. We are not going to suggest that we permit mistakes in our operations; quality control and the reduction of errors have been guiding lights of the industrial enterprise.

Secondly, we really cannot afford to do it. Society will not tolerate mistakes where previously there were none. So it seems at first glance that there is a block to the suggestion. There seems to be no possibility of having our cake of creativity and eating it too, at least in terms of reduced errors. However, if we can conceive of the total organization following the pattern of the motivation-hygiene theory, it appears then that the increase in the use of talent has to pervade the whole organization. Today, high-level personnel are frequently preoccupied with the responsibility for minimizing the errors of performance. Using these talented men in such a way restricts their creativity. If the responsibility for reduction of errors were given to lower-level people, this challenge would provide the motivator qualities for them and would also release the upper-level person from doing overly simple jobs. In this way, it is hoped that a constant job review, not only in terms of functions for company goals but also in terms of the nature of the jobs for human potentiality, would provide an increase in the total amount of motivators the company has to offer. In terms of the gain to the company, it would provide for greater creativity, perhaps less error and certainly less resistance to change. This prescription can apply today only to those who have some semblance of a human job. The completely rationalized worker, it is hoped, will be removed by automation. My concern is for the professional and managerial employees who have the most surplus potentiality, which seems to be headed for the scrap heap.

It can be hypothesized that, at the maximum, errors would increase without much harmful effect on production costs; and, at the other extreme, it can be predicted that errors might indeed be reduced. The most likely prediction from present evidence is that there would be a temporary reduction in errors, and possibly the error level would return to its previous mark.

How is this plan to be introduced? Obviously, all jobs lack growth potential at certain times, and the organization cannot move quickly enough to restructure jobs continually. There must be a lapse between outgrowing an old dimension and providing a new one. It is hoped that, as organizations develop along the lines presented here, this lapse can be anticipated. However, in the meantime, companies might very well entertain the idea of temporary sabbatical assignments of long-range value. Such sabbaticals have been given to blue-collar workers in order to stretch out work. Why could not sabbaticals be given to management people for purposes of personal renewal?

During management-development sessions that I conduct, I frequently ask conferees to list some of the pressing problems with which they are faced. After collecting the lists of problems, I make only one comment: "Why didn't you think about them before?" An obvious example is industry's failure to anticipate the civil rights movement. A number of years ago, this would have been a marvelous sabbatical assignment—resolving problems in hiring Negroes—for those companies that had a built-in system permitting such foresight. These sabbatical assignments may be as short as a few days or as long as a year; they do not have to be a continuous assignment, but may be a part-time sabbatical from meaningless jobs.

Another means of effectuating the ideas presented here would be to include in the periodic reviews of the effectiveness of work performance a simultaneous review of the growth potential of the job itself. We talk so much about two-way communication, and so often the two-way communication in a job-performance review can be reduced to the difference in opinions about how well a man has done his job. However, the employee has more desire to talk about the potential for growth of his job than about his performance.

Supervision must be altered to approximate the kind of direction we find in teaching hospitals between the teaching staff and the interns and residents. Here the intern or resident is systematically being given tasks that are to assist his growth as a physician. The staff physician's primary role is not only to make sure that the intern or resident is immersed in tasks that will insure his growth but also to supervise his actual performance. What would happen if our doctors in training were given psychological support and didactic teaching but debarred from ever seeing and taking responsibility for live patients with real complications? Certainly, this is one area where errors cannot be allowed; yet it is surprising that where life and death are at stake, as in hospital situations, this kind of supervision is permitted and fostered.

This is true despite the fact the hygiene rewards in hospitals are among the worst. There we find doctors who are dictatorial in their attitudes, quite contrary to accepted standards of supervision in modern industrial relations programs. We also find salaries at the lowest level, fringe benefits practically nil and the working conditions for the intern and resident staff among the worst in all organizations. But we also find available the greatest growth opportunities for people.

A hard look at some of the barriers, other than those implicit in the discussion so far, that restrict the conceptualizing and implementing of the concepts set forth in this volume may result in more freedom of action than appears possible.

Paradoxically, the leaping trend toward professionalism, characteristic of more and more occupations, is acting as a force restricting the enhancement of the motivators at work. Professionalism, once a sign of true competence and dedication to excellence in performance, has now become a synonym for gathering the harvest of the hygiene factors of status and money.

I recall with some nostalgia my own professional organization, the American Psychological Association, which once arranged for pleasant scholarly meetings and kept me informed of what my colleagues were doing. Today, it has become a large business bureaucracy dedicated to obtaining the recognition for psychology that is essential if psychologists are to share in the manna that a society with a huge psychological hunger is prepared to provide.

The number of occupations that are seeking professionalization is equal to the number of organizations that hold meetings. Those close to my own discipline bent on adding their names to the roster of status professions are social workers, nurses, speech therapists, training directors and personnel managers. The American Medical Association is the unhappy model for the newly emerging (and underdeveloped) professions. In the process, the motivator satisfaction, and in particular the pride of craftsmanship, is lost.

A further word is necessary concerning the role of the personnel or industrial psychologist when he stands as a barrier to the implementation of the concepts outlined in this book. The industrial psychologist, unfortunately, has been more a tool of the traditional establishment than a professional with his own orientation.

Of all the unlikely groups in industry that find it distasteful to consider the Abraham requirements of employees, strangely enough, many are in personnel positions, including those with behavioral science credentials. The general personnel manager has been so preoccupied with maintaining hygiene that he can be forgiven for seeing industrial relations with only one eye. Less forgivable, but still quite understandable, is the hostility of those with psychological training who are employed by industry either directly or indirectly via consultantships or as professors guiding the education of graduate students in the field. The barrier of the behavioral scientist is well illustrated by the psychological programs in industry that center on the use of testing and of human-relations training.

We will begin with the human-relations approaches. Obviously, they have become much more sophisticated than the earlier, primitive attempts to improve supervisory practice by lectures on human dynamics. Today, rather than listen to such lectures, managers are often required to participate in modified forms of group psychotherapy. Perhaps the most ubiquitious of the new approaches to improving interpersonal attitudes is sensitivity training. Within the frame of reference of this book, how do we view these programs, and in particular sensitivity training?

First, if sensitivity training was designed to ameliorate the ever recurrent hygiene problems of human relations, it is most worth while. It cannot be denied that improving the way people understand themselves and get along with others, trust and communicate with others, accept and empathize with others, cannot but have a beneficial effect on the hygiene side of man. However, when the programs go beyond this goal, and assume that the motivator solutions will emerge once human relations have reached an appropriate level—this becomes nonsense. As we have pointed out, hygiene needs are never satisfied, nor can they feed the motivator needs. Attempts to do this, conscious or implied, can lead to further damage to the organization and particularly to the employee.

I perceive just such an overemphasis on human relations, and the point is fast being reached of defining all human problems in industry as those of inadequate interpersonal skills. The approach now determines the professional analyses of existing problems, and sensitivity training is more and more a vested interest and/or security blanket for the psychologist as he participates in industry. The worst result is to detract from the motivator problems. Job enlargement is occupying very few behavioral scientists, while the clinical psychologists are multiplying in industry to deal with the "discovered" personal problems of managers. Not only are trained clinical psychologists and psychiatrists being involved, but programs have been established to train therapists without relevant background in either psychology or psychiatry. It does not take real professional training for one to become sensitive to the surface manifestations of human frailties, but it does take sound training for one to understand the phenomena. Any housewife can recommend aspirin for a headache—but take the headache to a physician and he will probably wish to conduct a total physical examination, complete with X rays. Chances are that the physician will still prescribe aspirin, but only after much more professional analysis and deliberation.

Not only does this overemphasis on human relations detract from "organic" problems, but it also often leads to the interpretation of immorality, dishonesty, lack of personal integrity, power striving, empire building and status seeking as interpersonal incompetence. Psychotherapy, of whatever form, has a very bad record in dealing with the reformation of character disorders. But it is precisely these amoral managers who may benefit most by sensitivity training, because they are taught the more subtle tools and understandings which they use for their own Machiavellian manipulations of people. In this regard, sensitivity training results in a rather vicious human-relations one-up-manship.

More frequently than not, interpersonal difficulties arise from the defensive reactions that people employ to mask their incompetence on the job and their professional and intellectual inadequacies. These, too, are not amenable to change by the improvement of interpersonal skills; on the contrary, such skills may be a means to reinforce their defenses. The ability to handle people becomes a cover for their concrete failures. We have enough administrators of this sort by natural selection, without adding to their ranks and attaching a "humanistic" label to their nefarious behavior.

Another group who "benefit" are the psychological voyeurs, the Peeping Toms who have never passed their preadolescent stage of peeping. To such people, the easiest point to sell is that the origin of problems is emotional weaknesses. Everyone is a prime target for this accusation. Every problem is treated with the universal remedy of better interpersonal skills. I sincerely hope I am overstating the case.

Empathy, acceptance, tolerance, understanding and the rest of the humanitarian dreams have been preached for thousands of years with little development in the purity of man's behavior. The hygiene part of the theory finds much corroboration in the records of man's past. You cannot really empathize with someone else. Your nervous system is as unique as your fingerprints, and therefore to try to fit yourself into someone else's skin is going to result in a bad fit. If, however, you assume that you do fit, your actions are necessarily going to be harmful to the other person. The same dangers apply to tolerance, love, trust and the other endless pleas for human acceptance. We should recognize, by now, that there is a vast indeterminacy in all human relationships.

Psychological testing is on less shaky ground. The test specialist has much solid accomplishment behind him and has earned the right to his influence in industrial selection and employee assessment. However, this influence has gone far beyond the specialist's acknowledged contribution. The examination of knowledge, general intellective ability and special aptitudes for selecting employees at the lower levels in industry and for the guidance of students in schools have more than proved their worth. But at the higher levels, these measures tend to lose their prognostic value, and the testers have accordingly moved into the "measurement" of personality characteristics of employees for advancement, as well as for employment selection. There has been much justified criticism of the results of personality testing, even if some has been uninformed. There is one criticism that I would like to reinforce. It seems to me that the occasional success of psychological assessment at the higher levels of jobs has been paid for by the enhancement of mediocrity in the majority of cases.

The transparency of so much of psychological assessment is continually being disguised by mysterious devices when the clinically trained psychologist is at work, and by befogging mathematical tricks when his hard-nosed brethren in psychometrics are involved. Wielding mathematics with little understanding of the human problems of people at work leads to comic and tragic consequences. Perhaps informed psychological understanding is too much to expect from the worst of this breed, but one could hope for a little common sense from them on occasion.

Personnel researchers are an offshoot of the specialist in psychometrics, and they share some of the same guilt. The psychological problems of industry have passed beyond their comprehension and skill; yet they flourish by retreating more and more into clever measuring devices, much like boys playing with toys, but unfortunately they are playing adult games. When the professional weight of these respected technicians is thrown behind the organizations' inherent inclination to define employees as Adam, then industry gains "scientific" sanction for further reducing the hope for Abraham's chances. In many respects, the joke is on these psychologists. They are partially accepted because the major purpose they serve is to give industry a more complete self-image of rationality by including personnel relations within its scope of approaching the world with the businessman's prized sense of objectivity. But in the process, Abraham still suffers.

An interesting barrier to the recognition of this problem at the managerial level is the general tendency to ascribe it solely to the blue-collar worker. The psychological trick of displacement in this instance is not very successful. The same denigration of human talent at the managerial and profession level, the same sacrifice of human performance and potentiality to insure that no one will fail or will make for unpleasantness, is obscured by this reference to the rank and file when acknowledging the lack of meaning in work. But, at the higher levels, the effects of the assembly line are accomplished, as we suggested earlier, by the overuse of rules and regulations and of rational organizational principles and by the insidious use of interpersonal skills. We find that more and more training and education are required to do less and less; there is more and more stress on environment and less and less on accomplishment. In the Russian study referred to earlier, the Soviet sociologists comment, "the widening of his [those doing meaningless work] mental horizons and the increase of his education does not improve, but rather worsens his attitude to work and it impels him to quit his job. In this case, the appeal to the social value of labor hardly helps, since other work is more useful to society due to its greater productivity." The Russians are simply corroborating, from their experience, that educating people more and more to do less and less is hardly a prescription for healthy industrial relations.

Perhaps the greatest single obstacle to action lies in the inability to conceptualize and to recognize that man lives at two separate levels and is motivated by two opposing needs. Obviously, we walk around with our hygiene and motivator needs wrapped in one package. Obviously, we do not separate what we do from the situation in which we do it. Obviously, we feel pain concurrently with happiness. Therefore, it becomes linguistically as well as experientially difficult, if not impossible, for people to conceive of their experiences as being made up of two diverging parts.

The physical sciences are no longer uncomfortable with the fact that the essential rationality of nature is opposed to man's direct perception of nature. Physical scientists do think practically in theoretical frames of reference. The physicist has little difficulty in practical applications of things that are beyond human comprehension when human comprehension is considered in terms of the primitive sensory mechanisms. Physical scientists deal with mathematical abstractions of reality that they cannot experience, but these abstractions reflect reality in a much more predictable fashion than do those expressions of human knowledge and implementation that stem directly from sensory and experiential considerations. Similarly, if man exists as a duality conceptually, even though this duality is not directly experienced, then the controlling human institutions will find it more fruitful to deal with human beings in the light of the conceptual view of man than the "sensory" view.

There is no theoretical barrier to the implementation of the dual nature of man. The studies reviewed in this book show that this concept can be demonstrated in real-life situations, and if it can be demonstrated, it should be possible to implement it.

There is now a spate of new research and literature that is reacting to personnel and managerial psychology which has too long tried to emulate the vast, short-term goals of the military. The new literature (while encompassing diverse problems, exhortations, solutions and conceptions) seems to have the common theme of emphasizing the motivator needs of man and the necessity for the personnel function of industry to become creative in finding ways to meet the motivator needs. Man is distinguished from all other animals in that he alone is a determiner. How strange that when it comes to the satisfactions of his unique needs for psychological growth, he finds himself a victim of outside determinisms and helpless in affecting the way he is utilized in work.

The short-term economic "necessities" cannot justify the larger economic loss and the denial of human satisfaction that the restriction of human talent inevitably costs. I might add that many of the barriers to fuller utilization of manpower that are "justified" by economic reasons are, in reality, devices of fearful and inadequate managers who are not prepared to meet the challenge of managing adults. The philosophy of management that prizes such men is changeable. We can select and train managers who operate through people's growth needs, rather than those who function through the manipulation of people's avoidance needs. We need a goal of industry that includes the expansion of manpower utilization, in addition to the expansion of productivity and profit. The acceptance of such a goal as basic will lead to the means for its implementation.

Not only does industry have a stake in the propositions put forth in this book but, it seems to me, society itself has still a greater stake in terms of its general mental health. In an examination of the past concepts of mental health, the chief consideration seems to be the alleviation of mental illness. These two concepts, mental illness and mental health, are quite separate. Mental health, as shown, relates to man's actualizing his Abraham nature. This actualization depends upon what man accomplishes, and the major area in which he acts as a determining individual is on the job. Therefore, industry becomes the prime resource for psychological income that is necessary to mental health, just as industry provides an influential environment that contributes to the alleviation of the psychological deficits of man that lead to mental illness. Eventually, the improper utilization of people in industry will have a deleterious effect on the mental health of society.

Just as a fever is a normal reaction to an infection, the behavioral fever that results from the improper definition of man will be considered an abnormal response rather than the logical consequence of the sick use of man. Simply speaking, if we look upon a fever as an unnatural reaction to an infection and institute procedures to get rid of the fever, not the infection, we will find ourselves dealing with increased and exacerbated symptomology.

An obvious characteristic of the mentally sick is their unadaptability, a constriction in their choices of behavior. The mentally well, in contrast, are more adaptable and therefore can choose alternative patterns of adjustment. When the two are in conflict, the result will be the conforming of the healthy to the maladjusted. The culture will thus reflect more the hygiene seekers' needs than those of people with positive mental health. This is another explanation of why society is more easily geared to the hygiene goals of people than to their motivator needs.

One of the tragedies of my profession has been the scientific sanctions that the social scientists, and psychologists in particular, have given to the normalization process of mental sickness. When these scientists discover, through their biased instruments, that man has a fever, they conclude that the fever is a normal attribute of human nature rather than a normal symptom of a sickness. The laws of psychology are too much the laws of symptoms, which are then ascribed to man's basic character. For example, the psychological "insights" into job attitudes from this orientation have suggested that the needs of blue-collar workers and of women are pretty much reflected by the job factors of wages, supervision, working conditions and other assorted hygiene factors. Indeed, these findings about lower-level workers are true.

From a survey of industrial research efforts reported in my book *Job Attitudes: Research and Opinion*, which encompassed almost a half-century of effort on the part of industrial psychologists, I have documented this difference between the blue-collar workers and their more fortunate white-collar brothers. But the reader will recall that, contrary to this established belief, the samples of blue-collar workers and women in the replications of the motivation-hygiene study appeared to be no different in their job attitudes from engineers, scientists and managers. Such differences as did occur were clearly attributed to the way in which these workers were used on the job.

Mentally ill people should have all the compassion and concern that a humanistic society can provide, but a sane society has to protect itself from the corruption of the mentally sick and from the further corruption by the mental health professional who goes beyond compassion and understanding to label pathological behavior as normal. We realize this when we lock up the traditional type of mentally sick person; we do so in order that he not infringe on the rights of the normal. But the mentally ill, in the motivation-hygiene sense, direct the operations of our industrial organizations to fit their restricted repertory of behavior and then receive "scientific" sanction from the industrial psychologist. We fail to realize that they are also infringing on, and reducing the potentiality of, the mentally healthy. Sooner or later, the company reaps the rewards of this normalization of the pathologic. Its goals become directed to the worker who is hygiene-oriented rather than to the worker who is motivator-oriented, and then the companies wonder why there is so little creativity and spirit in their organizations.

It is sometimes suggested that today's mental health problems stem from the fact that we are living in a much more complex society than has been known before. Perhaps society is no more complex, within its own frame of reference, today than in the past. I am sure that the idea that we are living in a more intricate and more ambiguous time has been bemoaned since the dawn of man. Ancient Egyptians, medieval people and contemporary man all have a kinship in sharing the feeling that the world is too complex for them. It is true that objectively we have made more scientific advances and have acquired more knowledge, but subjectively, from the standpoint of the psychological boundaries of the individual, life is no more complex than it has ever been. What has been changed, however, is the lead time to make corrections in the cybernetic systems by which man and nature operate.

In the past, man was fortunate in having sufficient time to make the necessary corrections for his survival and for giving him hope in survival. But today the lead time for man's biological survival has been drastically reduced to about fifteen minutes. In terms of man's spiritual need, the shortening of lead time is evidenced by the frenetic efforts of the leaders of our mystery systems to make adjustments in their messages and to readjust their institutions. "We want it now" suggests that lead time for correcting social problems has disappeared. We can no longer afford an improper view of man, not because an improper view leads to mistakes, but rather because there is too little time to develop another Renaissance that might give purpose, direction, hope, aspiration and a future to human beings.

In addition to the war on poverty, in all its forms, physical and psychic, the Great Society will not be realized until we wage a war against the denigration of Abraham. Impractical? So is the kind of life we now lead.

Appendix

First-Level Factors

AS HAS BEEN INDICATED, we define a first-level factor as an objective element of the situation in which the respondent finds a source for his good or bad feelings about the job. In this section we attempt to describe the criteria for each of our categories, so that the reader can understand what we mean when we refer to them in the discussion of our findings. These factors are listed not in the order of their importance but of their appearance in our coding scheme.

1. *Recognition.* The major criterion for this category was some act of recognition of the person speaking to us. The source could be almost anyone: a supervisor, another individual in management, management as an impersonal force, a client, a peer, a professional colleague or the general public. Some act of notice, praise or blame was involved. We felt that this category should include what we call "negative recognition," that is, acts of criticism or blame. In our subcategories we differentiated between situations in which rewards were given along with the acts of recognition and those in which there were no concrete rewards. Note that we had many sequences in which the central event was a certain act, such as a promotion or a wage increase, which was not itself accompanied by verbal recognition but which was perceived by the respondent as a source of feelings of

recognition. These sequences were coded under "recognition second level."

One might ask, since we had a separate category for interpersonal relations, where we coded recognition and where we coded interpersonal relations. The defining characteristic was the emphasis on the act of recognition or on the characteristics of interaction. When the story included statements characterizing the nature of the interaction between the respondent and the supervisor, peer or subordinate, we coded the sequence as a story involving interpersonal relations. When the emphasis was merely on the act of recognition, this was not done.

2. *Achievement.* Our definition of achievement included also its opposite, failure, and the absence of achievement. Stories involving a specifically mentioned success were put into this category, and these included the following: successful completion of a job, solutions to problems, vindication and seeing the results of one's work.

3. *Possibility of growth.* The inclusion of a possibility as an objective factor in the situation may sound paradoxical, but there were some sequences in which the respondent told us of changes in his situation involving objective evidences that the possibilities for his growth were increased or decreased. An illustration of this is a change in status that officially included a likelihood that the respondent would be able to rise in a company, or the converse. For example, if a man moves from a craftsman's position to that of a draftsman, the new status opens up a previously closed door; he may eventually rise to the position of design engineer or perhaps even of project engineer. When the respondent told us that this had been clearly presented to him as part of his change, then possibility of growth was certainly considered as a first-level factor. Similarly, when an individual was told that his lack of formal education made it impossible for him ever to advance in the company, "negative" possibility for growth was coded.

Possibility of growth, however, has another connotation. It includes not only the likelihood that the individual would be able to move onward and upward within his organization but also a situation in which he is able to advance in his own skills and in his profession. Thus, included in this category were stories in which a new element in the situation made it possible for the respondent to learn new skills or to acquire a new professional outlook.

4. *Advancement.* This category was used only when there was an actual change in the person's status or position in the company. In situations in which an individual transferred from one part of the company to another, with no change in status but with increased opportunities for responsible work, the change was considered an increased responsibility (for which we have a category) but not formally an advancement.

5. *Salary.* This category included all sequences of events in which compensation plays a role. Surprisingly enough, virtually all of these sequences involve wage or salary increases, or the unfulfilled expectation of salary increases.

6–8. *Interpersonal relations.* One might expect that interpersonal relations would pervade almost all of the sequences. They do play a role, necessarily, in situations involving recognition or changes in status within the company or company and management policies; however, we restricted our coding of interpersonal relations to those stories in which there was actual verbalization about the characteristics of the interaction between the person speaking and another individual. We set this up in terms of three major categories:

Interpersonal relations—superior
Interpersonal relations—subordinate
Interpersonal relations—peers.

Within each of these categories we used a series of subcategories, to describe various kinds of situations involving interaction between the person speaking and others. These subcategories would have enabled us to differentiate between the characteristics of interpersonal relationships that are purely social and those that are "sociotechnical," as defined by J. A. C. Brown. A sociotechnical story involves interpersonal relationships that arise when people interact in the performance of their jobs. A purely social story might relate interactions that take place during working hours and on the premises of work but are independent of the activities of the job. A coffee-break friendship or a water-cooler feud are examples. As it turned out, we had virtually no stories of the purely social kind. Whether this result was due in some way to the set produced by our interviewing instructions, whether this is a characteristic of the level of people to whom we spoke, or whether in fact the nature of extra-job interpersonal relationships in the plant does not play so great a role as has been assumed, it is not at present possible to determine.

9. *Supervision-technical.* Although it is difficult to divorce the characteristics of interpersonal relationships with one's supervisor from one's behavior in carrying out his job, it seemed to us that it was not an impossible task. We were able, with a high degree of reliability among independent coders, to identify those sequences of events that revolved around the characteristics of interpersonal relationships and those, classified under the category of supervision-technical, in which the competence or incompetence, the fairness or unfairness, of the supervisor were the critical characteristics. Statements about the supervisor's willingness or unwillingness to delegate responsibility, or his willingness or unwillingness to teach, would be classified under this category. A supervisor who is perpetually nagging or critical and a supervisor who keeps things running smoothly and efficiently might both be reported as factors in a sequence of events that led to exceptional feelings about the job.

10. *Responsibility.* Factors relating to responsibility and authority are covered in this category, which includes those sequences of events in which the person speaking reported that he derived satisfaction from being given responsibility for his own work or for the work of others or from being given new responsibility. It also includes stories in which there was a loss of satisfaction or a negative attitude toward the job stemming from a lack of responsibility. However, in cases in which the story revolved around a wide gap between a person's authority and the authority he needed to carry out his job responsibilities, the factor identified was "company policy and administration." The rationale for this was that such a discrepancy between authority and job responsibilities would be considered evidence of poor management.

11. *Company policy and administration.* This category describes those components of a sequence of events in which some over-all aspect of the company was a factor. We identified two kinds of over-all company policy and administration characteristics. One involved the adequacy or inadequacy of company

organization and management. Thus, a situation can exist in which a man has lines of communication crossing in such a way that he does not really know for whom he is working, in which he has inadequate authority for satisfactory completion of his task or in which a company policy is not carried out because of inadequate organization of the work.

The second kind of over-all characteristic of the company involved not inadequacy but the harmfulness or the beneficial effects of the company's policies. These are primarily personnel policies. When viewed negatively, these policies are not described as ineffective, but rather as "malevolent."

12. *Working conditions.* This category was used for stories in which the physical conditions of work, the amount of work or the facilities available for doing the work were mentioned in the sequence of events. Adequacy or inadequacy of ventilation, lighting, tools, space and other such environmental characteristics would be included.

13. *Work itself.* This category was used when the respondent mentioned the actual doing of the job or the tasks of the job as a source of good or bad feelings about it. Thus, jobs can be routine or varied, creative or stultifying, overly easy or overly difficult. The duties of a position can include an opportunity to carry through an entire operation or they can be restricted to one minute aspect of it.

14. *Factors in personal life.* As previously indicated, we did not accept sequences in which a factor in the personal life of an individual having nothing to do with his job was responsible for a period of good or bad feelings, even if these feelings affected the job. We did accept situations in which some aspect of the job affected the individual's personal life in such a way as to make the effect a factor in the respondent's feelings about his job. For example, if the company demanded that a man move to a new location in a community in which his family was unhappy, this was accepted as a valid sequence of events and was coded under the "personal life" category. Similarly, family needs for salary and other family problems stemming from the job situation were acceptable.

15. *Status.* It would have been easy to slip into the trap of inferring status consideration from other factors. For example, it

might be considered that any advancement would involve a change in status and ought to be thus coded. This was not done. "Status" was coded only when the respondent actually mentioned some sign or appurtenance of status as a factor in his feelings about the job. Thus, a person who spoke of having a secretary in his new position, of being allowed to drive a company car or of being unable to use a company eating facility gave us a story coded under this category.

16. *Job security.* Here again we were not dealing with feelings of security, since these were coded as second-level factors, but with objective signs of the presence or absence of job security. Thus, we included such considerations as tenure and company stability or instability, which reflected in some objective way on a person's job security.

References

Preface and Chapter 1

Eliot, T. S. *The Wasteland and Other Poems.* Faber and Faber, London, 1940.

Herzberg, F., *et al. The Motivation to Work.* John Wiley and Sons, New York, 1959.

Norton-Taylor, Duncan. "Businessmen on Their Knees," *Fortune Magazine,* October, 1953.

University of Michigan Institute for Social Research. *Discrimination Without Prejudice,* 1965.

Wall Street Journal, February 2, 1965.

Western Reserve University. Workshop in the Simplification of Dental Procedures, 1959.

Chapter 2

Adams, H. *Mont-Saint-Michel and Chartres.* Houghton, Mifflin Co., New York, 1933.

Artz, F. *The Mind of the Middle Ages.* A. A. Knopf, New York, 1953.

Freud, S. *Moses and Monotheism.* A. A. Knopf, New York, 1939.

Ganshof, F. L. *Feudalism* (translated by Philip Grierson). Longmans, Green, London, 1952.

Haskins, C. H. *The Renaissance of the Twelfth Century.* Harvard University Press, Cambridge, 1927.

Lot, F. *The End of the Ancient World and the Beginning of the Middle Ages.* A. A. Knopf, New York, 1931.

Lynd, R. S. *Knowledge for What?* Princeton University Press, Princeton, 1939.

Marx, K. *Capital.* Modern Library Edition.

Muller, H. J. *The Uses of the Past: Profiles of Former Societies.* Oxford University Press, New York, 1957.

Pico Della Mirandola, quoted by Ernst Cassier, ed. *Renaissance Philosophy of Man.* University of Chicago Press, Chicago, 1948.

Silberman, A. M. *Pentateuch with Rashi's Commentary.* Vol. I. Shapiro, Vallentine & Co., London, 1946.

Thomas Aquinas, quoted by Etienne Gilson. *Moral Values and the Moral Life: The Systems of St. Thomas Aquinas* (translated by Leo Richard Ward). B. Herder Book Co., St. Louis, 1931.

Chapter 3

Argyris, C. *Personality and Organization.* Harper & Bros., New York, 1957.

――――. Personal communication to author.

Babock, M. D., quoted by Reinhard Bendix. *Work and Authority in Industry.* John Wiley and Sons, New York, 1956.

Bendix, R. *Ibid.*

Copley, F. B. *Frederick W. Taylor, Father of Scientific Management.* Harper & Bros., New York, 1923.

Mayo, E. *The Social Problems of an Industrial Civilization.* Harvard University, Division of Research, Graduate School of Business Administration, Cambridge, 1945.

Roethlisberger, F. J. and Dickson, W. J. *Management and the Worker.* Harvard University Press, Cambridge, 1939.

Weber, M. *The Protestant Ethic and the Spirit of Capitalism.* Scribner's, New York, 1962.

Westminster Confession of 1647, quoted by Max Weber. *Ibid.*

Chapter 4

Fowler, H. *Curiosity and Exploratory Behavior.* Macmillan, New York, 1965.

Fromm, E. *Escape from Freedom*. Farrar & Rinehart, New York, 1941.

Hardin, G. *Nature and Man's Fate*. Rinehart, New York, 1959.

Hebb, D. O. "Drives and the Conceptual Nervous System," *Psychological Review*, 62, 1955.

Kleitman, N. *Sleep and Wakefulness*. Rev. ed. University of Chicago Press, Chicago, 1963.

Lilly, J. C. "Mental Effects of Reduction of Ordinary Levels of Physical Stimuli on Intact, Healthy Persons," *Psychiatric Research Reports*, 5, 1965.

Chapter 6

Herzberg, F. "Basic Needs and Satisfactions of Individuals," *Industrial Relations Monograph*, No. 21. Industrial Relations Counselors, Inc., New York, 1962.

———. "Motivation-Hygiene Concept and Psychotherapy," *Personnel Administration*, Jan.-Feb., 1964.

———. "New Approaches in Management Organization and Job Design," *Industrial Medicine and Surgery*, 31, 1962.

———. "The New Industrial Psychology," *Industrial and Labor Relations Review*, 18, 1965.

———. *Psychology and Work Simplication*. Western Reserve University, Workshop in the Simplification of Dental Procedures, 1959.

———. "Salary—a Dissatisfier," *Proceedings of the American Compensations Society*, Annual Meeting, 1965.

Herzberg, F. and Hamlin, R. "The Motivation-Hygiene Concept and Psychotherapy," *Mental Hygiene*, 47, 1963.

———. "A Motivation-Hygiene Concept of Mental Health," *Mental Hygiene*, 45, 1961.

Herzberg, F., Mausner, B., and Snyderman, B. *The Motivation to Work*. John Wiley and Sons, New York, 1959.

Chapter 8

Dunnette, M. and Kirchner, W. K. *Psychology Applied to Industry*. Appleton-Century Crofts, New York, 1965.

Ewen, R. B. "Some Determinants of Job Satisfaction," *Journal of Applied Psychology*, 48, 1964.

Fantz, R. "Motivational Factors in Rehabilitation." Doctoral dissertation, Western Reserve University, 1962.

Fine, S. and Dickman, R. *Satisfaction and Productivity*. Paper presented to American Psychological Association Convention, St. Louis, September, 1962. Available from authors at the Applied Physics Laboratory, The Johns Hopkins University.

Friedlander, F. "Job Characteristics as Satisfiers and Dissatisfiers," *Journal of Applied Psychology*, 48, 1964.

————. "Relationships Between the Importance and the Satisfaction of Various Environmental Factors," *Journal of Applied Psychology*, 49, 1965.

Friedlander, R. and Walton, E. "Positive and Negative Motivations Toward Work," *Administrative Science Quarterly*, 9, 1964.

Gibson, J. W. "Sources of Job Satisfaction and Job Dissatisfaction as Interpreted from Analyses of Write-in Responses." Doctoral dissertation, Western Reserve University, 1961.

Graglia, A. and Hamlin, R. *Effect of Effort and Task Orientation on Activity Preference*. Paper delivered at Eastern Psychological Association Meeting, Philadelphia, 1964.

Hahn, C. *Dimensions of Job Satisfaction and Career Motivation*. Reported in P. Schwarz. *Attitudes of Middle Management*. American Institute for Research, Pittsburgh, 1959.

Halpern, Gerald. *Relative Contributions of Motivator and Hygiene Factors to Over-all Job Satisfaction*. Paper presented to American Psychological Association Meeting, Chicago, September, 1965.

Hamlin, R. and Nemo, R. "Self-Actualization in Choice Scores of Improved Schizophrenics," *Journal of Clinical Psychology*, 18, 1961.

Haywood, C. H. and Dobbs. *Motivation and Anxiety in High School Boys*. Peabody Papers in Human Development, Vol. 1, No. 9, 1963.

Herzberg, F. "A Case Study of Attitudes to Labor in the Soviet Union," *Personnel Psychology*, Fall, 1965.

Herzberg, F. "The Motivation to Work Among Finnish Supervisors," *Personnel Psychology*, Winter, 1965.

Herzberg, F. and Hamlin, R. "The Motivation-Hygiene Concept and Psychotherapy," *Mental Hygiene*, 47, 1963.

——. "A Motivation-Hygiene Concept of Mental Health," *Mental Hygiene*, 45, 1961.

Herzberg, F., Mausner, B., Peterson, R., and Capwell, D. *Job Attitudes: Research and Opinion*. Psychological Service of Pittsburgh, 1957.

Kahoe, R. *A Developmental Study of Motivator-Hygiene Factors*. Peabody Papers in Human Development. George Peabody College for Teachers, 1963.

Saleh, S. *Report of "Pre-Retirement Study."* Ontario Department of Civil Service, 1964.

Saleh, S. and Otis, J. "Sources of Job Satisfaction and Their Effects on Attitudes Toward Retirement," *Journal of Industrial Psychology*, 1, 1963.

Sanford, N. "Will Psychologists Study Human Problems?," *American Psychologist*, 20, 1965.

Sanvold, K. "The Effect of Effort and Task Orientation on the Motivator Orientation and Verbal Responsivity of Chronic Schizophrenic Patients and Normals." Doctoral dissertation, University of Illinois, 1962.

Schwarz, P. *Attitudes of Middle Management Personnel*. American Institute for Research, Pittsburgh, 1959.

Vroom, V. and Maier, N. "Industrial Social Psychology," *Annual Review of Psychology*, 12, 1961, 413–446.

Wernimont, P. and Dunnette, M. *Intrinsic and Extrinsic Factors in Job Satisfaction*. Paper presented at Midwestern Psychological Association, St. Louis, May, 1964.

Yadov, V. A. "The Soviet and American Worker: Job Attitudes," *Soviet Life*, January, 1965.

Zdravomyslov, A. and Yadov, V. A. "A Case Study of Attitude to Labor," *Problems of Philosophy*, Moscow, 4, 1964.

Chapter 9

Hegedüs, A. *Optimization and Humanization on the Modernization of Management Systems*. Hungarian Academy of Science, 1965.